D1598230

Canon Law and
Cloistered Women

Studies in Medieval and

Early Modern Canon Law • Volume 5

Canon Law and Cloistered Women

Periculoso and Its Commentators

1298–1545

Elizabeth Makowski

The Catholic University of America Press
Washington, D.C.

For Balbina Kasianowicz and Helen Rose Banaszynski

Copyright © 1997
The Catholic University of America Press
All rights reserved
Printed in the United States of America

The paper used in this publication meets the minimum requirements of
American National Standards for Information Science—Permanence of
Paper for Printed Library materials, ANSI Z39.48–1984.
∞

Library of Congress Cataloging-in-Publication Data
Makowski, Elizabeth M., 1951–
     Canon law and cloistered women : Periculoso and its
commentators, 1298–1545 / by Elizabeth Makowski.
          p.   cm.—(Studies in medieval and early modern
canon law ; v. 5)
     Includes bibliographical references and index.
     1. Convents (Canon law)—History.   2. Monasticism and
religious orders for women (Canon law)—History.   3. Nuns—
History.   4. Monasticism and religious orders for women—
History—Middle Ages, 600–1500.   I. Title.   II. Series.
LAW
262.9′2—dc20
96-43744
ISBN 0-8132-0884-X (alk. paper)

Contents

Acknowledgments

I wish to acknowledge the assistance of the rare book staff of the Burke Library, Union Theological Seminary, and of Columbia University's Law School Library. Special thanks to Daniel Williman, Charles Donahue Jr., F. Donald Logan, and Walter Simons, for generously sharing the fruits of their own research.

Particular mention is due Robert Somerville, who tirelessly directed the dissertation from which this book emerged, and Caroline Walker Bynum, whose insights and criticism helped to improve it. I would also like to thank Kenneth Pennington, the editor of this series, and James A. Brundage, who first introduced me to the study of canon law, and to whom my debt of gratitude seems to increase with each year.

Abbreviations

DDC   *Dictionnaire de droit canonique.* Ed. R. Naz. 7 vols. Paris: Letouzey et Ane, 1935–65.

DMA   *Dictionary of the Middle Ages.* Ed. Joseph Strayer. 13 vols. New York: Scribner's, 1982–89.

DNB   *Dictionary of National Biography.* Ed. Leslie Stephen and Sidney Lee. Oxford: Oxford University Press, 1917– .

DTC   *Dictionnaire de théologie catholique.* Ed. A. Vacant et al. 15 vols. Paris: Letouzey et Ane, 1909–50.

Mansi   *Sanctorum conciliorum nova et amplissima collectio.* Ed. Giovanni Domenico Mansi. 31 vols. Florence–Venice, 1759–98.

NCE   *The New Catholic Encyclopedia.* 15 vols. New York: McGraw Hill, 1967.

Schulte, QL   J. Friedrich von Schulte. *Die Geschichte der Quellen und Literatur des canonischen Rechts von Gratian bis auf die Gegenwart.* 3 vols. Stuttgart: F. Enke, 1875–77; rpt. Graz: Akademische Druck- u. Verlagsanstalt, 1956.

Canon Law and
Cloistered Women

Bibliotheca Apostolica Vaticana Borghese 7, *Liber Sextus* folio 56v.

Introduction

In 1298 Pope Boniface VIII (1294–1303) published a decree that transformed pious counsels to nuns—women bound by solemn profession of the three vows of poverty, chastity, and obedience, and living under an accepted monastic rule—into universal church law.[1] Referred to as *Periculoso,* the first word of the Latin text, this decree was the first papal legislation to require strict enclosure of nuns of every order throughout the Latin Church. Boniface included this decree as title 16 in the third book of his *Liber Sextus,* an official compilation of papal legislation that formed part of the collected law of the Western Church, the *Corpus Iuris Canonici.* Because of its inclusion in a legal collection that contained material relevant to some of the most important issues of the era—issues such as conciliarism—some of the most influential jurists and academics of the fourteenth and fifteenth centuries who wrote commentaries on the *Liber Sextus* included a discussion of *Periculoso.* Although it proved difficult to enforce, sustained

---

1. *Periculoso* applied exclusively to nuns—canonically the only "truly religious" women. See chap. 1 for a discussion of the quasi-religious alternatives available to thirteenth-century women. For an overview of the evolution of the notion of solemn profession, and the distinctions between vowed virgins, widows, and others see the entries "Nuns" and "Vows" in the *NCE.*

legal interest in *Periculoso* resulted in its re-enactment, with the addition of stern penalties for its violation, at the Council of Trent (1545–63).

Periculoso began by announcing that thenceforth all nuns, no matter what rule they observed and no matter where their monasteries were located, were to be perpetually cloistered. With the exception of the contagiously ill, who might threaten the lives of their sisters by remaining among them, nuns were under no circumstances to break the law of enclosure, either by leaving their monasteries or by inviting unauthorized persons into them. Except for mendicant communities, convents whose resources were inadequate to support their members were to accept no further postulants, in order to avoid taxing their limited resources. Once enclosed, nuns, even abbesses, were not to risk exposure to worldly temptations. Boniface commanded temporal lords, as well as bishops and other prelates, to permit abbesses and prioresses to do homage, swear fealty, and conduct any other legal transactions on behalf of their monasteries through the agency of a proctor whenever possible. Finally, he authorized bishops and other prelates to enforce the provisions of *Periculoso*, even in convents immediately subject to the protection of the Holy See, and warned that any who disregarded his admonitions would incur not only ecclesiastical but also secular penalties.[2]

Although rules governing entrance to, exit from, and activity in the cloister—areas of a monastery reserved for the exclusive use of monks or nuns—were a recognized element of monasticism from the earliest days of the church, scholars see *Periculoso* as a watershed in the history of women's religious life.[3] Earlier cloister regulations had, when ap-

2. *Liber Sextus* 3.16.1; See Appendix 1 for the full Latin text and for my translation.

3. Virtually all of the scholars working on cloister regulations for women say this in no uncertain terms. See for example: Micheline Pontenay de Fontette, *Les religieuses à l'âge classique du droit canon,* introduction and 60; Gerard Huyghe, *La clôture des moniales des origines à la fin du XIIIe siècle,* 99–101; James R. Cain, "Cloister and the Apostolate of Religious Women," 243–80, esp. 267; Jean LeClerq, "La Clôture," 366–76, esp. 371; Mother Maria Caritas McCarthy, *The Rule for Nuns of St. Caesarius of Arles,* 65; Craig Harline, "Actives and Contemplatives," 544. Note that complete bibliographic information is provided for these and all subsequent references in the bibliography.

plied, been similar for monks and for nuns, and there had been a general appreciation of the need to bend the rules of enclosure for the economic and spiritual good of monastic communities.[4] After 1298, if we take *Periculoso* literally, strict active and passive cloistering of nuns— prohibitions involving not only exit from, but also entrance by unauthorized persons into, the monastic confines—was to be observed perfectly, under threat of excommunication. This novel papal policy, when enforced, entailed radical changes in the discipline of female religious houses. Strict enclosure of nuns threatened to undermine the economic stability of these communities. It required drastic changes in the relationship between convents and their benefactors, many of whom were relatives of the nuns, thus threatening to deprive women's religious houses of one of their most vital and reliable sources of revenue. It severely limited the capacity of nuns to solicit funds from outside benefactors, to conduct schools within conventual precincts, or to engage in any kind of revenue-producing labor outside the cloister. The furnishing of room and board (in effect, retirement homes) to laywomen, no matter how respectable, was also prohibited by Boniface VIII's decree. Since, at the same time, the pope insisted that communities of nuns be fiscally sound and that convents limit the number of women admitted to them, *Periculoso* had the effect of diminishing their importance for the Christian community. There was, furthermore, no equivalent legislation set down for monks.[5]

With stringent enclosure laws Boniface VIII seemed to be trying to do for nuns throughout Europe what earlier reforming popes like Gre-

4. Jane Tibbetts Schulenburg, "Strict Active Enclosure and Its Effects on the Female Monastic Experience ca. 500–1100," 51–86, makes a good case not only for initial similarity in cloister regulations but also for the general laxity of early observance. See also: Penelope Johnson, *Equal in Monastic Profession*, and the work of Constance Berman, for France ; for medieval England, Eileen Power, *Medieval English Nunneries* is still valuable, especially for its documentation on *Periculoso* and actual practice.

5. Soeur Marie-Amélie Le Bourgeois, "Dieu aime-t-il les murs?" aptly summarizes the evolution of Western church law on enclosure: "la clôture, qui au départ n'était qu'un moyen, une précaution pour des hommes et des femmes qui s'engageaient dans le 'célibat pour le Royaume' devint en effet peu à peu, et ceci exlusivement pour les femmes, une fin en soi à laquelle toute la vie religieuse féminine avait à être subordonnée," 19.

gory VII had attempted to do for the clergy. By strictly enforcing sac-
erdotal celibacy, the eleventh-century papacy had set the priesthood
clearly and distinctly apart from the laity. By prescribing strict cloister
regulations, Boniface VIII gave nuns a status separate not only from
male religious and laywomen, but also from the growing number of
quasi-religious female communities competing for, and often winning,
the support of the pious. That some of these communities were feared
to harbor heretics who challenged the very foundations of papal authority could surely have served as an additional motive for stern regulation.[6]

Although historians of religious life frequently cite *Periculoso* as a
watershed for medieval women, only Micheline Pontenay de Fontette
and Gerard Hyghe refer to it in any detail. Both of their works, moreover, as well as that of Jane Tibbetts Schulenburg, end before the Bonifacian legislation took effect. Studies such as Soeur Marie-Amelie Le
Bourgeois' analysis of the impact of enclosure regulation on the new
teaching orders of the seventeenth-century bracket, but do not inves-
tigate, the late Middle Ages.[7]

Yet it is precisely the late medieval period that recent scholarship
on religious women singles out as an era of significant, and sometimes
dramatic, shifts in the character of Christian ideals, many with special
relevance to women. Clarissa Atkinson, for instance, has pointed out
that, after the thirteenth century, there was an increasing tendency
among hagiographers to interpret virginity in moral and psychological
rather than physical terms. Thus, the woman whose life was charac-
terized by purity and humility, the wife as well as the mother, was still
capable of preserving "true" virginity.[8]

Nor was the questioning of traditional ideas confined to issues of

6. These threats will be dealt with in chapter 2. Note especially, the followers of one Guglielma of Milan in the late thirteenth century. Guglielma is reported to have condemned Boniface VIII as a counterfeit pope and declared
that ecclesiastical revival would hinge on the election of an all-woman hierarchy.

7. Power, *Medieval English Nunneries,* deals with enforcement of *Periculoso* in
the later medieval period, but only in England.

8. Clarissa Atkinson, "Precious Balsam in a Fragile Glass: The Ideology of
Virginity in the Later Middle Ages."

sexuality. The efficacy of solemn vows and withdrawal from the world, of sharp distinctions between lay and religious, active and contemplative life, all were debated notions in the last medieval centuries. The doubts raised by these debates were significant enough, according to Caroline Walker Bynum, to warrant labeling the fourteenth and fifteenth centuries a separate stage in the history of Christian ideas and institutions—a stage, moreover, in which lay piety in general took on the characteristics formerly attributed only to female piety.[9]

Like the fate of *Periculoso* in the fourteenth and fifteenth centuries, the sources used in this study remain underexplored.[10] Yet while the work of academic jurists in the earlier, more innovative, period of canon law evolution might be more attractive to modern scholars, the give-and-take between papacy and academy was far from over in this, the so-called post-classical era. When Boniface VIII formally promulgated the *Liber Sextus,* and with it *Periculoso,* he addressed his papal bull not to the church hierarchy but to the doctors and scholars of the universities—evidence of the crucial role that academic canonists continued to play in the development of church law. Professional interpretation by the lawyers often gave rise to further papal legislation, which, in turn, was again the subject of university teaching.

Like their predecessors, canonists throughout the fourteenth century usually gave these interpretations in glossed texts, that is, they explicated or elaborated key words and phrases found in the text of a law. A gloss was often brief, sometimes little more than a listing of cross-references to related texts, and often written in the margins of manuscripts.[11] For the *Liber Sextus,* Johannes Andreae (d. 1348), author of the standard gloss *(Glossa Ordinaria)* set a basic pattern that oth-

---

9. Caroline Walker Bynum, *Holy Feast and Holy Fast,* introduction.

10. Nothing like Stephan Kuttner's invaluable *Repertorium der Kanonistik (1140–1234),* or Paul Fournier and Gabriel Le Bras, *Histoire des collections canoniques en Occident depuis les fausses décrétales jusqu'au Décret de Gratien,* exists for the "post-classical" (after about 1250) period in the canon law. Indeed, Gabriel Le Bras once claimed that the epoch of the Great Schism provided no material for a historian of the canon law.

11. For details about the various genres of canonistic writing see Antonio Garcia y Garcia, "The Faculties of Law," 394–97. For an overview of medieval canonical development, see James A. Brundage, *Medieval Canon Law.*

ers followed, but they by no means slavishly imitated him. "Glossators" expanded or abbreviated comments on particular passages, added citations and cross-references to earlier legislation, and modified the remarks of their predecessors as personal feeling and experience, breadth of legal learning, and penchant for allusion dictated. Some assembled a collection of glosses on only one part of the corpus. Such a collection, written in the order of the text but without the text alongside it, was called an *apparatus. Lectura,* or lecture notes sometimes taken by canonists while still law students and so reflecting the opinions of their own professors, were also common.

In the late fourteenth century the treatise became a more important form of academic legal literature. Much longer than a gloss, a treatise *(tractatus)* is a detailed and closely focused treatment of a special topic of the law, completely independent of a specific text. Because it was not tied to any single title of a codification, the treatise, like the *summa,* became indispensable to practitioners. Students and judges, who were faced with an ever-increasing body of legal literature, clearly appreciated having at their disposal works that synthesized legal opinion and that professed to be comprehensive guides to what had been stated elsewhere on the same subject.

Canon Law and Cloistered Women is a study of *Periculoso* and the legal comment that its publication occasioned. It begins with a discussion of the religious climate of the last decades of the thirteenth century, with emphasis on those areas of special relevance to nuns and to the pope as legislator. A look at the law proper follows. Chapter 2 discusses the circumstances in which the pope drafted his sweeping statement and explores the precedents and possible motives for the decree. Chaper 3 charts the transmission of *Periculoso* to local ordinaries (those in charge of supervising the nuns within their jurisdictions), as well as to academics across Europe.

Chapters 4 through 6 correspond to the three chronological periods (each with its characteristic concerns), in which *Periculoso* was commented on by some of the most eminent jurists of the age. Chapter 4 deals with the first or formative era of canonical comment that ends with the publication, in 1305, of Joannes Andreae's standard gloss *(Glossa Ordinaria);* chapter 5 treats the second phase, in which the writers concerned themselves less with the theological or moral implications of Boniface VIII's legislation than with juristic implications of *Periculoso*—this phase extends into the fifteenth century; represented especially by the treatise, a third stage features writers who lingered over the legal technicalities, whether of enforcement or circumvention, of *Periculoso*. Chapter 6 deals with this period, the *terminus ad quem*, 1545, marking the opening of the Council of Trent—the council that strongly reaffirmed, and added sanctions to, *Periculoso*.

These substantive chapters on the commentarial literature are analytical as well as descriptive. They focus primarily on comparisons among the words that the canonists chose to gloss (noting, as well, the words that they did not choose to comment on) and pay special attention to glosses on the word ''chastity'' and to the rich material about monks scattered throughout the texts. They describe stylistic variation among commentators, since such variation in style often highlights departures from common opinion. The legal and biblical citations and literary allusions with which the canonists decorated their texts are followed up whenever possible.

No matter how rich the academic literature, no matter how useful it may be for enhancing the intellectual and social history of the time, commentarial literature sheds little light on practical questions of enforcement. Was *Periculoso* accepted by local communities across Europe? Was it enforced by ordinaries? These, of course, are complex questions that would require one or more additional studies to answer, but the final chapter of this book provides some tentative answers for one specific place and time: late medieval England. While preliminary work on cataloging church court records on the Continent and in England suggests that there is fertile ground for investigation elsewhere, the larger volume of published material for medieval England, as well as the special ties between Crown and church officials seeking to control unauthorized exits from monasteries, colored the choice of venue.

Because English court practice was profoundly influenced by English canonists, chapter 7 presents the work of two of the most famous jurists (both were practicing lawyers as well as theorists) of fourteenth- and fifteenth-century England: John Acton and William Lyndwood. With the conclusions of these jurists in mind, the evidence from bishops' registers, the legislation of regional synods, and the letters that fourteenth- and fifteenth-century popes directed to the English Church, are examined in an attempt to gauge the extent to which English canonical theory concerning *Periculoso* was actually worked out in practice.

"Clausura" declared Cardinal Bellarmine, *"inchoata est Ecclesiastico instituto a Bonifacio VIII."*[12] Inspired by an ancient ecclesiastical ideal, and largely constructed from relevant contemporary legislation, *Periculoso* was nevertheless a novelty, a unique piece of legislation that tried to alter institutional religious life. Prescribing strict enclosure for all nuns throughout Christendom, Boniface VIII strove for uniformity of observance and devised mechanisms of enforcement that would cut across national boundaries. Yet it was those who commented on and/ or attempted to carry out his directives who ultimately affected the extent to which the pope's grand vision would be fulfilled. Whether exclusively as theorists, or as practitioners as well, the canonists of the later Middle Ages left us a wealth of detail, allusion, and argument. This book attempts to do justice to part of that legacy.

12. See page 122 of the conclusion of this book for the full quotation and citation.

O N E

Background—The Religious Climate in the
Late Thirteenth Century

Modern historians who have treated the issue of claustration of nuns in any depth differ in perspective but agree about two things: first, that some form of enclosure has been part of the monastic ideal for nuns in the West from a very early date and, second, that while there was great variety in the articulation and in the observance of cloister rules among communities of nuns throughout the Middle Ages, those rules gradually increased in strictness. References to the cloistering of women are found as early as the fourth-century letters of St. Jerome and in legislation coinciding with the founding of the first communities of pious women in Rome.[1] Although the sixth-century *Regula ad moniales* of St. Caesarius of Arles was the first rule for women to impose the cloister as such, cloister regulations for nuns in the West date back to the advice of St. Augustine to consecrated virgins to remain in their homes, separate from the world.[2]

Admonitions that nuns maintain strict cloister reappear in a variety

1. Schulenburg, "Strict Active Enclosure," 52–53. Cain, "Cloister," 254.
2. Huyghe, *La clôture*, 19.

of early medieval sources—in the rules of Aurelian, bishop of Arles (d. 555), and Donatus, bishop of Besançon (d. 658), and in important Carolingian reform legislation—yet, as recent research shows, those admonitions were more often than not ignored.[3] While the medieval church placed progressively greater emphasis on the ideal of strict claustration for nuns from 500 to 1000 A.D., it took long centuries before such unequal strictures evolved into something like uniform law.[4] Not only were the great double monasteries of seventh-century Gaul unenclosed, but they were also ordinarily governed by the abbess.[5] Although Carolingian legislation did indeed tend to interpret the Benedictine Rule more rigorously for nuns than for monks by requiring cloistering for the former, such efforts proved to be premature; in the tenth century, with local families exploiting monastic revenues, rules were considerably eased.[6]

Strict cloister was insisted upon in the charter of the first Cluniac monastery for women at Marcigny (issued by Pope Urban II in 1095), and in the writings of such important reformers as Peter the Venerable, Ivo of Chartres, and the German Cistercian monk Idung of Prüfening, yet even in the later Middle Ages custom and need tempered legalism. Injunctions to observe enclosure were counterbalanced by more accommodating practice, and nonenclosed communities of nuns existed side by side with their more strictly confined sisters throughout the thirteenth century.[7] The resistance that thirteenth-century abbots faced when trying to effect enclosure of would-be Cistercian affiliates living under less confining regulations illustrates this situation.[8] Even

3. See below; Michel Parisse, *Nonnes au Moyen Age*, 184, argues that the cloister was an unattainable ideal before the eleventh century; Jean Leclerq, "Medieval Feminine Monasticism," 59, observes that, before the late medieval period, laws on enclosure of nuns were "neither universal, nor strict, nor largely observed."
4. Schulenburg, "Strict Active Enclosure," esp. 77–79.
5. Suzanne Wemple, *Women in Frankish Society*, 159–63.
6. Ibid., 173.
7. Johnson, *Equal in Monastic Profession*, 159. Penny Gold, "The Charters of Le Ronceray d'Angers," 122–32. Parisse, *Nonnes*, 182–86.
8. Sally Thompson, "The Problem of the Cistercian Nuns," 234–41. Huyghe, *La clôture*, 76–87; see also chapter 4 of this study for a discussion of Cistercian cloister regulations and their influence on *Periculoso*.

when a community had fully accepted enclosure, economic need sometimes took precedence over its steady observance.[9]

For centuries then, although nuns in Western Europe enjoyed a *de facto* economic and administrative liberty (whether motivated by legitimate economic and spiritual needs or distaste for rigorous enclosure rules), they appear to have been steadily if not consistently directed toward a more uniform and stricter observance of long-standing admonitions about enclosure. At the end of the thirteenth century, Boniface VIII attempted to complete the process and to eradicate all flexibility of cloister rules. There could be no doubt that his demand for the strict enclosure of all nuns of every order throughout Christendom had the potential to affect the lives of many religious women. Yet ironically, by 1298 it was also clear that it would no longer affect them all. By the time of *Periculoso*'s publication, a "women's movement" had been afoot in Western Europe for nearly a century. That movement had ushered in forms of religious life for women in addition to, and often in sharp constrast with, that of the traditional nun to whom *Periculoso* spoke.

In the early Middle Ages being a nun had been the only formalized religious role for women; further, for all its importance, it had been available only to a relatively small aristocratic population.[10] Nuns certainly continued to be important in the late thirteenth century, for the wandering preachers of the eleventh and twelfth centuries, whose attractiveness to women was well noted by contemporaries, founded monasteries for their female followers.[11] The new orders of the twelfth and thirteenth centuries such as the Premonstratensians, Cistercians, and Franciscans also had numbers of women in their ranks.[12] But af-

9. William Jordan, "The Cistercian Nunnery of La Cour Notre-Dame de Michery," 311–20.

10. Wemple, *Women in Frankish Society,* 164–65, notes that there was some variation in pre-Carolingian monasticism; Johnson, *Equal in Monastic Profession,* 16–17.

11. Men like Norbert of Xanten (d. 1134) and Robert of Arbrissel (d. 1117); see Brenda Bolton, "Mulieres Sanctae," 141–43, for an overview. The monastic foundations that were made helped ensure that there would not be bands of itinerant *women* evangelists—something that all twelfth-century preachers deplored.

12. Ibid. Chapter 2 will deal with more of the specifics in the Cistercian rule.

filiated women's houses strained the resources of the new orders with their demand for clergy to provide *cura monialium* (that is, spiritual direction and sacramental needs), and these orders attempted to limit if not to end admission of women.[13] The Premonstratensians decided to exclude women after 1198; in 1228 the Cistercian General Chapter formally tried to limit their responsibilities to previously incorporated nunneries and declared that the order would not in future provide spiritual guidance to any additional groups of women.

Alongside the traditional Benedictine nunnery and the often strife-ridden female monasteries of the new orders then, there began to be entirely new opportunies for women in thirteenth-century religious life. Some of these opportunities were quickly categorized by the Church as heretical. Scholars still debate the extent to which women were attracted to movements such as the dualist Cathars, the anticlerical Waldensians and Humiliati, or the antinomian Free Spirit, but women do seem to have been drawn to participate in movements that, at least in their formative periods, accorded them opportunities for religious leadership.[14] The Franciscan chronicler Salimbene, for example, described the actions of women as well as men in a 1284 gathering of a group of enthusiasts known as the Apostles; the roughly

13. The analysis of the religious climate of the twelfth and thirteenth centuries that saw a succession of male orders struggling with the task of providing for the spiritual care of large numbers of devout women was first put forward by Joseph Greven, *Die Anfänge der Beginen,* and subsequently elaborated by Herbert Grundmann, *Religiöse Bewegungen im Mittelalter.* This analysis provided the theoretical framework, or point of departure, for work as diverse as those of Ernest McDonnell, John Freed, and Brenda Bolton.

14. The argument that women were overrepresented in heresies is still not resolved; see for instance: Gottfried Koch, *Frauenfrage und Ketzertum im Mittelalter;* Eleanor McLaughlin, "Les femmes et l'hérésie médiévale: Un Problème dans l'histoire de la spiritualité." There is much literature on heresy in the late medieval period; see for example: Malcolm Lambert, *Medieval Heresy,* which is a synthesis of research on popular heretical movements in Western Europe from the eighth through the fifteenth centuries; R. I. Moore, *The Origins of European Dissent;* Robert Lerner, *The Heresy of the Free Spirit in the Later Middle Ages,* which deals in part with the way in which Beguines were implicated in this heresy, which was closely related to orthodox mysticism. If not overrepresented, women were frequently more vulnerable to attack as heretics, given their lack of ecclesiastical regulation and theological training.

contemporary Guglielmites—a sect that might have been especially nettlesome to Boniface VIII—believed in a leadership composed *exclusively* of women.[15]

Responding to impulses that were similar to, if not exactly the same as, those at the heart of some of the heretical movements, orthodox quasi-religious groups of women also emerged in the thirteenth century.[16] In northern Europe, especially the Low Countries, there were the Beguines, women who in marked contrast to nuns took no permanent vows and, at least initially, had no complex organization or rule, and no stable endowment.[17] They dedicated themselves to living poor, chaste lives and supported themselves by manual labor. The tertiaries of southern Europe, especially Italy, were a parallel phenomenon.[18] Attaching themselves to mendicant friars, Franciscan or Dominican, these women also lived lives of charity and austerity in pursuit of an evangelical ideal. They often continued to live with their families, but sometimes formed loosely structured communities.

Since the early part of this century, historians have tried to account for the emergence of these new types of female religious life. Karl Bücher's view, that they represented a protest movement of the poor and downtrodden, has now largely been discredited by research that shows that women who joined the Beguines or who became tertiaries often came from the new bourgeoisie or from a lower nobility associated with the towns; far from seeking to share in the accumulation of wealth and luxury, their ideal was to renounce it—theirs was a spiritual rather than an economic motive.[19] While generally agreeing that

15. R. W. Southern, *Western Society and the Church in the Middle Ages,* 276; for the Guglielmites, see chapter 2 of this study.

16. These impulses include bypassing of clerical authority, extreme asceticism, and affective religious response. See the work of Caroline Bynum, especially "Women Mystics and Eucharistic Devotion in the Thirteenth Century," 119–50, and "'. . . And Women His Humanity': Female Imagery in the Religious Writing of the Later Middle Ages," 151–80, in *Fragmentation and Redemption.*

17. Beguines also existed in France, the Rhineland, and Switzerland. See Walter Simons,"The Beguine Movement in the Southern Low Countries: A Reassessment," which contains an overview of recent scholarship.

18. Elizabeth Petroff, *Consolation of the Blessed,* 26–27; Bolton, *Muliere Sanctae,* 144–45; Cain, "Cloister," 273–78.

19. Karl Bücher, *Die Frauenfrage im Mittelalter;* for a reevaluation see Grund-

the choices that quasi-religious women made reflected a genuine spiritual purpose—the beguinage, for example, being a new and attractive alternative to the cloistered monastery—some scholars have argued that the resistance of the new orders to female affiliations stimulated the rise in quasi-religious women's groups.[20] Others have seen a demographic surplus at the center of the movement: beguines, heretics, and tertiaries were simply women for whom a lack of eligible men, or prohibitively large dowries, made marriage impossible.[21]

Whatever the explanation for the "women's movement," the variety of religious roles for women in the late thirteenth century was indeed remarkable, and *Periculoso* seems to have been an attempt to cordon off nuns (the most traditional and generally the most well-born women religious) from that growing welter of groups, sects, and individuals.[22] The very impulse to establish such lines of demarcation—in fact, the impulse to segregate orthodox from marginal—appears to have been a prime characteristic of the era of *Periculoso*.[23]

Yet stricter enclosure regulations, whether for nuns in the new orders or those remaining in the traditional Benedictine houses, had the further effect of undermining the symmetry that had existed between monks and nuns in the early Middle Ages. Although tradition still upheld (and the canonists would still express) the view that there was a unity of purpose in the monastic vocation and that monks and nuns were in theory doing the same spiritual work, monks had long had greater flexibility in observance of the rules of enclosure. They continued to have that flexibility, and now the friars, the new religious ideal of the age, were no longer, even in theory, required to act in the same milieu. Increased emphasis on strict enclosure of nuns at a time

---

mann, *Bewegungen,* and more recently, Freed, "Urban Development and the 'Cura Monialium' in Thirteenth-Century Germany."

20. For the "religious surplus" explanation see Greven, *Anfänge;* Grundmann, *Bewegungen;* Southern, *Western Society;* Bolton, "Mulieres Sanctae."

21. See Bücher, *Frauenfrage;* David Herlihy, "Women in Medieval Society."

22. On the social class of thirteenth-century nuns see Freed, "Urban Development," 324: "Only the wealthy could afford the poverty of the cloister."

23. Penelope Johnson, *Equal in Monastic Profession,* 260–64, has a good summary of some of these developments. See also treatments such as John Boswell, *Christianity, Social Tolerance, and Homosexuality,* and Saul Brody, *The Disease of the Soul: Leprosy in Medieval Literature.*

when the friars moved, as Christ had, in the bustle of the city could
only point up the anachronistic distinctiveness of the former; it made
nuns increasingly dependent on male religious as well. Not only the
conduct of their mundane business affairs but also their spiritual needs
required ever more priestly intervention. Gone were the days of the
great abbesses of the early Middle Ages, who routinely preached and
blessed their nuns. If nuns still claimed such powers for themselves in
the thirteenth century—and some did—they were increasingly condemned for it. When Dona Sanchia Garcia (1207–30), the abbess of
the Cistercian house of Las Huelgas, presumed to hear confessions
from and to bless her novices, Pope Innocent III vigorously denounced
her actions; in 1228 monastic confession, which could be heard by the
abbess, was officially replaced by the sacrament of penance, which required the services of a priest.[24]

Ironically, it seems that, as the number of priests among monks
(and friars) increased, the traditional fear of "pollution" by contact
with women—even holy women—grew as well.[25] Increasingly dependent on priest-monks, the differences rather than the similarities between monks and nuns began to be most evident. These differences
would in turn breed more distinctions—practical, theological, and
legal.[26]

24. Sally Thompson,"The Problem of the Cistercian Nuns," 238; Johnson,
Equal in Monastic Profession, 260. Johnson, 160 and 226, notes that not only were
nuns prohibited from celebrating mass—a consideration that affected patron-
age, since people often gave contributions for masses for the dead—but they
were also increasingly burdened with costs incurred for priestly ministrations
to the community. See also Constance Berman, "Women as Donors and Patrons
to Southern French Monasteries in the Twelfth and Thirteenth Centuries." On
the elimination of quasi-clerical roles see also, Caroline Bynum, *Holy Feast and
Holy Fast,* 21–22, and *Jesus as Mother,* 15.

25. Petroff, *Consolation,* 23; Johnson, *Equal in Monastic Profession,* 161–62. It
must be remembered that friars and monks did, no matter what their scruples,
provide spiritual direction to many nuns and quasi-religious; see for example
the statistics in Freed, *Urban Development.*

26. For example, we will see the commentators on *Periculoso* identifying virtues relevant exclusively to nuns; as Joseph Lynch, *Simoniacal Entry into Religious
Life from 1000 to 1260,* has shown, even the notion of simony applied differently
to nuns than to monks—entrance dowries for nuns continued to be common
well after they had been banned as simoniacal (1130) and eliminated from

No discussion of the period in which *Periculoso* took shape would be complete without mention of the papacy and the volatile ecclesiastical politics of the time. In the last decades of the thirteenth century, the papacy too was reaping a harvest from seeds sown centuries earlier. The process of centralization of power, originally of such importance to the growth and operation of the church, had by this time reached a point of diminishing returns. Caught up in secular affairs and the massive amount of judicial business that its developed legal system attracted, popes had taken to themselves more power than they could easily exercise. This rank overdevelopment was accompanied by no corresponding growth in papal status, but rather by the beginnings of a decline in papal prestige and even demoralization among the clergy. "Because all roads led to Rome," Geoffrey Barraclough noted, "no initiative remained with the local prelates, and the diocese—formerly the basic unit of church government—became an empty shell. Constantly harried by the Roman curia, deprived of initiative, weakened in the face of their subordinates, the bishops became apathetic, lost heart or turned their energies in other directions."[27]

As early as the Fourth Lateran Council, in 1215, there were signs that the papacy was not satisfying the majority of clergy and that there might be sustained clerical opposition to any further increase in power or prerogative. These portents were indeed troubling, particularly when coupled with anti-sacerdotal feelings on the part of the laity that could, and did, erupt into heretical denials of the validity of a materialistic hierarchy. Disaffection of the clergy meant that the church became truly a body divided and that, when a conflict arose between king and pope, as between Boniface VIII and Philip the Fair, one segment of the clergy would always support the royal viewpoint and might

---

practice in male houses (by the early thirteenth century). Educational discrepancies that grew up in the thirteenth and fourteenth centuries because nuns were not allowed into universities were noted by scholars as far back as Lina Eckenstein, *Women under Monasticism,* 480; Caroline Bruzelius, "Hearing Is Believing: Clarissan Architecture, ca. 1213–1340," 83–91, has recently noted the extent to which the architecture of convents (for Poor Clares, the female counterpart to the socially active, transient, Franciscan friars) was influenced by the imperatives of strict enclosure.

27. Geoffrey Barraclough, *The Medieval Papacy,* 125–26.

even be relied on to develop the rationale for monarchical defense of the right order of the church within their realms.[28] Several factors accounted for the dissatisfaction among clergy as well as laity in the late thirteenth-century church, not the least of which was the use of spiritual means to achieve temporal ends.

Evidence suggests that the thirteenth-century papacy had begun to overuse and thus to diminish the effectiveness of its main spiritual weapon, the sentence of excommunication. As R. W. Southern observed, "Most of the great Italian cities suffered papal excommunication at some time or other in the thirteenth century, sometimes for periods of several years. They dealt with the situation in a spirit of commercial calculation, as they might have dealt with a shortage of food or raw materials. It was a considerable nuisance, but it was not at terrible disaster. The ultimate papal weapon had ceased to be a sanction on a different level from any other."[29] In need of revenue for wars and diplomacy, the popes had also begun to reserve for their own use more and more appointments to benefices throughout Europe. Income could be had from those willing to pay for important appointments, and a large and impressive bureaucracy could be supported by non-resident livings flung out across national boundaries, but absentee prelates did little to enhance the spiritual credibility of the papacy. In addition, since the popes could make their appointments effective only with the consent of secular rulers, direct papal intervention in diocesan elections actually strengthened that external brake on the unfettered exercise of papal power, the authority of kings and princes.

Although late thirteenth-century popes believed that "the secular sword is in the power of Peter," they realized that the plenitude of power, which conferred upon them supreme political as well as ecclesiastical power, could not be exercised directly.[30] Political power had to be delegated to secular rulers who, as kings and emperors demonstrated with increasing regularity, acted more often as independent

28. Ibid., 134.

29. Southern, *Western Society,* 135; Southern also notes the overuse of papal indulgences, 136–43.

30. Quoted from the bull *Unam Sanctam,* November 1302, as translated in Brian Tierney, *Crisis of Church and State,* 188–89.

agents than as agents of the pope. In their exhausting attempts to establish control of the emperor, chief among the pope's political dep-
uties, the thirteenth-century popes had begun to realize that if they
were to tame independent secular rulers they would have to use all of
their own weapons, temporal and spiritual. Success in the international political arena thus exacted a dual price: it drove the papacy to
near bankruptcy and it demeaned it as well. The measures popes took
to defend and rule the papal states made them indistinguishable from
other, secular, rulers.

When Benedict Gaetani was elected to the papacy in 1294, he
brought his own set of problems to the still-mighty yet unstable office.
The first problem revolved around the election itself. Boniface VIII had
been chosen by the cardinals to fill the vacancy left by the resignation
of his predecessor, Celestine V. Since there was no clear precedent in
canon law for the resignation of a pope, the issue, hotly debated in
treatises and by the masters of the University of Paris, bedeviled the
pope throughout his reign.[31] Boniface's election was ultimately deemed
valid, but its irregularity served the pope's enemies well. The Spiritual
Franciscans were among these enemies, since one of the first acts of
Boniface VIII as pope had been to rescind Celestine V's concession
allowing the disgruntled Spirituals to establish themselves as an au-
tonomous order. Boniface compounded his "crimes" by imprisoning
Peter Morrone (the erstwhile Celestine), ostensibly to guard against
schism, and in 1296, by declaring the Spirituals to be heretics.[32] Another local enemy, one with whom the Spirituals would find common
cause, was the Colonna family. In his attempts to increase Gaetani land
holdings at the expense of this powerful aristocratic family, Boniface
VIII used both excommunication and crusading tactics against them.
Finally—and most significantly for the future of the papacy as an institution—Boniface clashed with the king of France, Philip the Fair.

31. And after his life as well, considering the posthumous trial that Philip
the Fair wished to hold for Boniface VIII, whom he accused of heresy, simony,
and murder (of Celetine V); see Tierney, *Crisis*, 174. See the still-unrivaled biography by T. S. R. Boase, *Boniface VIII*, for analysis of the chief events of his
reign; also useful: Charles Wood, ed. and trans., *Philip the Fair and Boniface VIII*;
Charles Wood, "Boniface VIII," *DMA* 2, 323–24.

32. See chapter 2 for more on Celestine, the Spirituals, and the Colonna.

Fashioned in 1296 as a response to the protests of French Cister-cians to royal taxation, the bull *Clericis laicos* prohibited all secular tax-ation of the clergy without prior papal approval. Philip the Fair re-sponded to this assault on his autonomy by issuing a royal ordinance forbidding all export of currency and precious metals from France—export that the papacy sorely needed for warfare, diplomacy, and the support of its massive bureacracy. Facing threats of a coalition made up of the Spirituals, their supporters among the Colonna, and Philip, Boniface capitulated. In the bull *Etsi de statu* of July 1297, the pope conceded that when clear necessity dictated (Philip was at this time at war with England), a king could tax his own clergy without the consent of the pope.[33]

By 1297 then, Boniface had suffered a clear defeat by Philip the Fair. He had, in effect, recognized the right of a sovereign to one aspect of national policy-making without reference to papal overlordship. Yet, in November of that same year he proclaimed a crusade against the Colonna; he had the cardinals from that family imprisoned and their family estate at Palestrina razed and sown with salt. And his fortunes continued to improve. In 1298, in addition to publishing the monu-mental and enduring *Liber Sextus,* he had once again been called to the center of European diplomacy, this time acting as arbitrator between the warring kings of England and France.[34] By the Jubilee year 1300, inspired by the sight of tens of thousands of the faithful streaming into Rome to receive the papal indulgence, Boniface VIII would once again be convinced of his right to seek to translate papal authority into ju-risdiction; confident of the power, if not the invulnerability, of the Vicar of Christ.

Periculoso was promulgated in an age of paradox. In the late thir-teenth century, roles for religious women that gave them power and position by virtue of their office—as abbess of an important double

33. There has been much written on the second phase of the conflict be-tween Philip and Boniface—a conflict that occasioned the publication of the famous bull *Unam Sanctam* as well as the calling of the first Estates General. See generally, Boase, *Boniface VIII;* Tierney, *Crisis;* Joseph Strayer, *The Reign of Philip the Fair;* Wood, ed. *Philip the Fair and Boniface VIII.*
34. Southern, *Western Society,* 148.

monastery for instance—seem to have been shrinking and the unofficial ones growing; celibate priesthood and clerical status assumed unpredecented importance, yet the ordinary things of the world, lay activity and everyday symbols, appear to have appealed to the popular imagination. Nuns were being subjected to ever-stricter enclosure regulations, while the new spiritual ideal for the age, as embodied in the friars, was one of an active apostolate. One of the great lawyer popes, Boniface VIII was working from a base of power unknown in an earlier period, while also being enmeshed in national politics which threatened to undermine that power forever. *Periculoso* asserted papal plenitude of power and called on secular rulers and the bureaucratic resources of a vastly enlarged papal machine to do a job that to some (even within the hierarchy) must have seemed undoable, and to others, unnecessary. It is to a closer examination of that document, itself paradoxical, that we now turn.

T W O

Circumstances of Composition: Models
and Motives

In the 1605 edition of the *Glossa Ordinaria* (standard gloss) to the
Liber Sextus, commentary on *Periculoso* is preceded by a description
of the circumstances that purportedly occasioned the decree. A certain person in the presence of Boniface VIII asked the pope to tell him
how nuns ought to live; *Periculoso* was the pope's extemporaneous reply.[1]

As difficult as it may be to credit the characterization of *Periculoso*
as an unrehearsed answer to an anonymous petitioner, this vignette
provides virtually the only known historical attempt to explain why
Boniface VIII composed his decree ordering the strict enclosure of all
nuns. Since *Periculoso* does not appear to have been a decretal letter—
a papal rescript sent in response to a specific query or dispute—and
since it appears for the first time not in the papal registers but as a
canon in the *Liber Sextus,* the immediate reasons for its issuance may

1. Joannes Andreae, *Glossa Ordinaria* to *VI* 3.16.1 in *Corpus iuris canonici* 4
vols. (Venetiis: Apud Iuntas, 1605) "Quidam constitutus in presentia Bonifacii
VIII quesivit ab eodem, 'Sanctissime Pater, vellem a vobis informari in quo statu
debeant vivere moniales?' Respondet Romanus Pontifex quod . . .'"; there follows a paraphrase of *Periculoso.* This "explanation" for the decree occurs in none
of the earlier printings of the ordinary gloss that I have looked at.

never be known. We can, however, hazard some speculations based on a study of related papal documentation, especially letters, as well as the evidence bequeathed us about groups of women who might have particularly piqued the interest, and provoked the ire, of the pope.

The letters of Boniface VIII, as found in the papal registers for the years immediately preceding the promulgation of *Periculoso,* illustrate the pope's paternal concern for nuns living the cloistered, well-regulated, life deemed appropriate to their sex and vocation; they show his willingness to mitigate the harshness of cloister rules when warranted. They also demonstrate the fact that Boniface lost no time in denouncing behavior that failed to meet his standards.

Mulieres quas vagari, for example—a constitution from the first year of his pontificate and one which also found its way into the *Liber Sextus*—decrees that women are not to be forced (either by apostolic letters or by those of legates) to appear against their will in order to give testimony personally in a court of law.[2] Under all but the most exceptional circumstances, a notary or even the judge himself should be sent to record a woman's testimony, rather than require her presence in court. Lest magistrates assume that these considerations appropriate to Christian women at large might suffice for religious women as well, Boniface concludes: "And surely religious women who ought to remain cloistered are not to be called or compelled to leave their monastery or cloister to appear personally before a judge for any reason, even if they are willing to do so."[3]

2. *Les registres de Boniface VIII* ed. G. Digard, M. Faucon, A. Thomas (Bibliothèque des écoles françaises d'Athènes et de Rome: Paris, 1884–1939) *Mulieres quas vagari* entry #774, April 8, 1295, 262 Lettres Curiales Premiere Annee; the constitution enters the *Liber Sextus* as *VI* 2.1.2; Potthast #24061.

3. "Ceterum feminae religiosae praesertim quae debent sub clausura morari, extra suum monasterium vel clausuram non vocentur ad iudicium vel trahantur ex quavis causa personaliter, etiamsi ad hoc voluntas accederet earundem"; note that here, as in *Periculoso,* Boniface VIII follows a precedent already established by the reign of Justinian. In *Novel* 123, chapter 27, Justinian decreed: "Whenever a suit is brought, and a legal summons is served, or an execution is issued in any civil proceeding whatsoever, either public or private, against a clerk, a monk, a nun, or a monastery, and especially against a monastery of women, We order that notice of it shall be given without the commission of any injury, and with all due respect under the circumstances, and

Cited by Joannes Andreae in his influential ordinary gloss, the relevance of *Mulieres quas vagari* to *Periculoso* was fully recognized by early commentators.[4] But other, less general, register entries also point up the pope's early concern to show that he considered the terms "religious women" and "cloistered women" to be synonymous. In 1295, for instance, Boniface gave the Franciscan convents of Waterbeach and Gracedieu in England exempt status, emphasizing the fact that both of these houses of Poor Clares be strictly enclosed communities; he had approved the rule of Waterbeach, founded in 1294, earlier that same year.[5] Clearly adumbrating *Periculoso,* the pope monitored the number of new admissions allowed into female monasteries in order to insure their solvency and obviate the need for worldly contact. In April 1296 he sent a letter cautioning the bishop of Nievre to guard against depleting the resources of the monastery of Fontevrault and cavalierly approving new admissions.[6] In harsh terms Boniface upbraided the nuns of Holy Mary of the Virgins in Venice for fraternizing with the priors and monks of Saint Mark, giving rise to discord and scandal.[7] In October 1296 the pope ordered a Dominican inquisitor in Lombardy to place the unruly Benedictine nuns of that province under perpetual enclosure.[8] He alleged that the nuns had merited this ruling because of the regularity with which suspect persons were allowed to enter, and the nuns themselves to leave, their monastery.

Orthodox nuns fallen into laxness aroused the pope's indignation and required immediate correctives—such as the swift application of cloister regulations—but the blatant flaunting of orthodox conventions,

---

that the nun or the hermit who is sued shall not be taken from his or her monastery, but an attorney shall be appointed to answer in the case." *Corpus iuris civilis,* ed. Paul Krueger, Theodor Mommsen, et al., as trans. S. P. Scott, 17 vols. (New York: AMS Press, 1973) vol. 17, 95.

4. Joannes Andreae, *Glossa Ordinaria* to *VI* 3.16.1 ad v. *fraudem & tractari.*

5. *Les registres de Boniface VIII* entries #457, August 31, 1295, Potthast #24176, and #458, August 31, 1295, 162 Lettres Communes Première Année, Potthast #24177; ibid., entry #659, August, 1295, 228, Potthast #18600.

6. Ibid., entry #1031, April 24, 1296, 358 Lettres Communes Deuxième Année.

7. Ibid., Lettres Communes Première Année entry #283, July 1295, 101.

8. Ibid., Lettres Communes Deuxième Année entry #1396, October 1296, 507.

not to mention doctrine, provoked a far sterner response. In 1296, Boniface published his constitution *Nuper ad audientiam,* which aimed at combating a clear and present danger to orthodoxy engendered by women.[9] Following introductory paragraphs, in which the pope admits of the ever-present threat of heresy and its ultimate inability to vanquish the Catholic Church, he recounts the errors into which an unnamed group, recently come to his attention, has fallen. Setting themselves up against the Church of Rome, the women of this sect teach, claim to have the right to hear confessions and to absolve from sin, conduct obscene nocturnal rituals, preach and misuse clerical tonsure.[10] Claiming that their authority derives not from a corrupt church but solely from the Holy Spirit, they deceive with their errors, "piercing the hearts of simple folk with their poisonous darts."[11] Wishing to provide a suitable remedy to this situation, to abolish "the insanity of such a great evil," Boniface VIII publically condemns the sect as heretical. He decrees that none are to aid its members, overtly or secretly, and that inquisitors are to be sent out to quash the spread of its depravity.[12]

While no definitive connection has been established, a very good argument can be made for linking *Nuper ad audientiam* to the late thirteenth-century Italian movement known as the Guglielmites.[13] Iden-

9. *Bullarium Romanum, Nuper ad audientiam* bull IX vol. 4, 134–35.

10. "Accepimus namque, quod nonnullae personae se contra sanctam catholicam Ecclesiam Romanam erigentes, etiam sexus foeminei, dognatizant, se ligandi et solvendi claves habere, poenitentias audiunt et a peccatis absolvunt, conventicula non solum diurna faciunt, sed nocturna, in quibus de suis pravitatibus conferunt, et de erroribus conveniunt in id ipsum, et praedicare praesumunt; tonsura clericali contra ritum Ecclesiae abutentes, Spiritum Sanctum se dare per impositionem manuum mentiuntur, et exhibendam soli Deo [deest aliquid, forsan reverentiam, venerationem] et non alteri, cuiuscumque fuerit conditionis dignitatis et status."

11. ". . . qui sagittas pestiferas cordibus simpliciorum infligunt."

12. "Ecclesiarum vero praelatis, et etiam inquisitoribus haereticae pravitatis, authoritate apostolica institutis ubilibet et instituendis imposterum, districtius iniungentes, ut contra tales, sicut contra haereticos, auxiliatores, consilatores, receptatores et fautores eorum debitum sui officii diligentius exequantur . . ."

13. See in particular the analysis by Stephen E. Wessley, "The Thirteenth-Century Guglielmites: Salvation through Women," in *Medieval Women,* ed. Derek Baker, 289–303; although the Guglielmites condemned Boniface VIII by name

tified with the Spiritual Franciscans and their champion, Peter John Olivi, the Guglielmites were an outstanding example of a woman-directed challenge to vested male authority in general, and to Boniface VIII's authority in particular.

The movement sprang up in the late thirteenth century, inspired by a woman—sometimes claimed to have been a Bohemian princess—named Guglielma of Milan.[14] Guglielma claimed that she was the incarnation of the Holy Spirit who would, upon her death and bodily ascent into heaven, send the Holy Spirit back to her disciples. She is reported to have declared that, in order to revitalize ecclesiastical authority, both pope and cardinals needed to be women and that one of Guglielma's disciples, Manfreda, would be the next successful papal claimant. Manfreda's papacy, in turn, would herald a final age of Christian unity in which all infidels would be converted.

As extreme as such apocalyptic claims sound, Guglielma was not unique in making them. As "part of a continuous development of thirteenth-century enthusiasm," the Guglielmites incorporated the popular motifs of *ecclesia spiritualis, imitatio Christi,* and *vita apostolica.*[15] The idea of an immanent new age of the Holy Spirit to supersede that of the Son and the Father, originally preached by the Cistercian abbot Joachim of Fiore (d. 1212) had become a compelling doctrine for many.[16] Guglielma's biography, modeled on the life of Christ, found echoes in the *vitae* of saints such as St. Francis.[17] Even the notion of a female incarnation of the Holy Spirit was not unique to the Guglielmites: women might be particularly equipped to usher in the new age, predicated as it was on a completely renovated church.[18]

---

as a pretender to papal power, as *pseudopapa,* Wessley does alert us to the fact that *Nuper ad audientiam* might have been directed against "several other groups," n. 8, 291; see also: Jo Ann McNamara, "*De Quibusdam Mulieribus:* Reading Women's History from Hostile Sources," in *Medieval Women and the Sources of Medieval History,* ed. Joel Rosenthal.

14. T. S. R. Boase, *Boniface VIII,* 116.

15. Wessley, "The Thirteenth-Century Guglielmites," 292.

16. Ibid; see also: Jo Ann McNamara, "*De Quibusdam Mulieribus:* Reading Women's History from Hostile Sources," 237–58, esp. 238 and 246, for Joachim's possible connection to the Cistercian cult of Guglielma.

17. Wessley, "The Thirteenth-Century Guglielmites," 295–96.

18. McNamara, "*De Quibusdam Mulieribus,*" 245–46, mentions three four-

Yet if the extremist claims of Guglielma and her followers were of a piece with other enthusiastic movements of the late thirteenth century, they were in one respect of peculiar concern to Boniface VIII. After the death of Guglielma in 1281, her followers condemned Boniface VIII as a pretender to papal power.[19] This denunciation, moreover, affected all of Milan: the Guglielmites claimed that, because he had been appointed by Boniface, Franciscus Fontana of Parma, archbishop of Milan from 1296 to 1308, was unable validly to exercise his duties.[20]

Furthermore, while his immediate predecessor Celestine V (Peter Morrone) had been hailed by many enthusiasts as the *papa sanctus* of the new age, Boniface VIII was particularly vulnerable to the Guglielmite charge that he was the *pseudopapa*. Not only had Celestine V still been alive when Boniface claimed the throne, but Boniface, fearing unwonted zealotry, had authorized the "detention" of the ascetic hermit-pope until his death (to which some said Boniface contributed).[21] Since Celestine V had been a decided advocate of the Spiritual Franciscans, Boniface faced sustained hostility (even in death) from pro-Spiritual forces, who were sometimes in league with the French, sometimes aligned with the powerful Colonna family.[22] All of his enemies in turn capitalized on the incongruous events surrounding his elevation to the papacy. Whether the charge of inauthenticity was leveled by the Colonna or by the Guglielmites, the pope's swift repri-

---

teenth-century women, Prous Boneta, an anonymous English virgin, and Margarita d'Arco, who claimed to be bearers, or manifestations, of the Holy Spirit.

19. Wessley, "The Thirteenth-Century Guglielmites," 298.

20. Ibid.; see also McNamara, "*De Quibusdam Mulieribus*," 248.

21. Boase, *Boniface VIII*, 73; for Celestine generally, see: Peter Herde, *Cölestin V.* Boase notes that Celestine had actually consulted "the expert legalist" Benedict Caetani on the question of his resignation, yet rumors of the foul play continued to circulate, 49.

22. Boase, *Boniface VIII*, 44–49. Celestine released imprisoned Spirituals and granted them the right to secede from the order—privileges Boniface VIII quickly canceled; on the relations between the powerful Roman Colonna family and the Spirituals, see 167–71. The Colonna charged that Boniface VIII had obtained Celestine's resignation by fraud and that he had subsequently murdered the hermit-pope; these charges became part of the libellus in Boniface VIII's posthumous trial conducted by Philip IV of France—protector of exiled Colonna cardinals.

sals were a measure of his repeated, if unsuccessful, attempts to coun-
ter it.[23]

However striking (and nettlesome) their claims, the Guglielmites
were nevertheless a fringe group, short-lived and decidedly small in
numbers.[24] The burgeoning quasi-religious communities of laywomen
throughout Christendom posed a much greater potential threat to
church discipline. Although technically orthodox in their observance,
women within these informal communities were unrestrained by
monastic rules and therefore were mistrusted by the hierarchy. It was
commonly argued by the canonists that if they were left unregulated,
pious laywomen were liable to become the abettors of anti-clericalism
or even overt heresy. This was certainly the attitude encountered by
the most prominent group of quasi-religious laywomen in northern
Europe, the Beguines.[25] Since they lived without permanent vows or
enclosure, the Beguines were coming under increasing attack from
ecclesiastical authorities.[26] Given the popularity of the movement, as
well as the hierarchical antipathy it evoked, there is every reason to
assume (but no direct evidence to confirm) Boniface VIII's knowledge
of Beguine activities. Even if he had lacked such personal knowledge,
however, his suspicions about lay female piety could have been well

23. Ibid., 177; Boase recounts the pope's crusade against the Colonna. According to his 1299 bull, the rebel family's headquarters at Palestrina were to
be razed and the ruins sprinkled with salt—a measure of Boniface VIII's fury.
Wessley, "The Thirteenth-Century Guglielmites," 302, reports that three Guglielmite sectaries were put to death by the inquisition and that Guglielma's remains were exhumed and burned.

24. Wessley, "The Thirteenth-Century Guglielmites," 302, mentions forty-
six sectaries at the time of their condemnation in 1300.

25. Ground-breaking studies of the Beguines, such as Herbert Grundmann,
*Religiöse Bewegungen im Mittelalter: Untersuchungen über die geschichtlichen Zusam-
menhange zwischen der Ketzerei, den Bettelorden und der religiösen Frauenbewegung im
12. und 13. Jahrhundert,* and Ernest McDonnell, *The Beguines and Beghards in
Medieval Culture,* have been overshadowed by a vast amount of recent scholar-
ship. An overview of this research is provided by Walter Simons, "The Beguine
Movement in the Southern Low Countries: A Reassessment." See also Andreas
Wilts, *Beginen im Bodenseeraum.*

26. Persecution of the Beguines began in earnest after the Council of
Vienne's 1312 condemnation, see: Grundmann, *Religiöse Bewegungen im Mittelalter,* chapter VI; Simons, "The Beguine Movement . . . ," 96–101; *DMA,* 161.

corroborated closer to home. Once again, the pope would have needed to look no further than Milan.

Inspired by the notion of an apostolic life combining manual labor, active charity, and contemplation, the Humiliati of Milan had crafted a program of life similar to that of the Beguines. Channeled by Pope Innocent III into a semi-monastic, and hence more easily supervised organization, the Italian Humiliati of the late thirteenth century consisted of cloistered, communal and tertiary branches.[27] In Milan, as elsewhere, both men and women belonged to the Humiliati, but since women were forbidden the actions most evocative of the *vita apostolica*—wandering and preaching—the Humiliati had a special appeal for them. As Humiliati tertiaries in particular, Italian women who would otherwise have had no alternative to cloistered convent life could continue to live in the world and engage in active charity while having access to spiritual guidance.

As the example of the Milanese Humiliati demonstrated, however, even when lay women were subjected to organizational strictures as rigorous as those imposed by Innocent III, they remained vulnerable to the lure of theological novelty. Not only did the Milanese house of Biassono provide shelter for the Guglielmite leader (and proposed future pope) Manfreda de Pirovano, but it also became a recruiting ground for the sect: six Humiliati sisters of the house ultimately joined the Guglielmites.[28] The implications might not have been lost on Boniface VIII.

Circumstances surrounding the composition of *Periculoso* remain obscure; precedents for the decree, both legal and literary, are easier to identify. When Boniface VIII composed his constitution, he incorporated elements of ecclesiastical rulings on the enclosure of nuns dating from at least as far back as the sixth century; he also found precedents in legatine and papal decrees promulgated within his own lifetime.

Caesarius of Arles's *Rule for Nuns (Regula ad moniales)* was the earliest rule written specifically for women and also the first to impose the

27. *Medieval Women's Visionary Literature*, ed. Elizabeth Alvilda Petroff, 231
28. Wessley, "The Thirteenth-Century Guglielmites," 298.

cloister upon them.[29] Writing for a small community of nuns in his diocese, the bishop of Arles (504–42) sought a practical means to attain his spiritual ideal: a contemplative life lived out by consecrated virgins. While this ideal had been a part of Christian tradition from the earliest centuries, Caesarius's pragmatic regulations, including his cloister provisions, made it viable in less than irenic times.[30] Indeed, the particularly detailed nature of his provisions has convinced at least one scholar that "though there is no direct historic continuity traceable between Caesarius' cloister law in 534 and the first universal imposition of the cloister on nuns by canon law in 1298, Caesarius' law contains all the elements which the Church officially adopted eight centuries later, and it must have influenced its long slow development."[31]

The parallels between *Periculoso* and the cloister rules contained in Caesarius's *Regula ad moniales* are, in fact, easy to discern. First, the *Rule for Nuns*, like *Periculoso*, is gender-specific. Although Caesarius's legislation for men, his *Rule for Monks*, contains a general prohibition against monks going out of, and women entering into, the monastery, his regulations for nuns are full of particulars for the maintenance of enclosure.[32] If a girl desires to renounce the world and to "escape the jaws of the spiritual wolves by the help of God, she must never, up to the time of her death, go out of the monastery, nor into the basilica, where there is a door."[33] The abbess is to hold the keys to the monastery entrance, and never to allow it to be opened without her permission.[34] Doors formerly used are to remain sealed off, and the main entrance vigilantly attended by the doorkeeper.[35]

Furthermore, Caesarius recognized that economic self-sufficiency (*Periculoso*'s stipulation that a monastery be able "to sustain its members with goods or revenues and without penury") was a necessary precondition for the maintenance of such strict cloister regulations. He

29. For an introduction to the rule as well as a translation of it, see: Mother Maria Carita McCarthy, *The Rule for Nuns of St. Caesarius of Arles.*

30. McCarthy, *The Rule for Nuns,* 28–30; 60–61. See also, Cain, "Cloister," 252–54.

31. McCarthy, *The Rule for Nuns,* 65.

32. Ibid., 62–63 and n. 72.   33. Ibid., chap. 2, 171.

34. Ibid., chap. 59, 189–90.   35. Ibid., chap. 73, 204.

stipulated that the economic security of his nuns be guaranteed by
alienation of some diocesan holdings in perpetuity—a stipulation that
Caesarius excluded from his *Rule for Monks.*[36]

Second, the *Rule for Nuns* resembles Boniface VIII's legislation in its
emphasis on passive as well as active enclosure. Except for the provisor
(the priest who acted as procurator and almoner) and clergy ministering to the spiritual needs of the nuns, men were not to enter the
cloister. "When the roofs have to be mended, or the doors and windows
have to be replaced, or something of this sort has to be repaired, skilled
workmen and slaves to do any such work may come in with the provisor if necessity requires it; but not without the knowledge and permission of the mother."[37] Secular women and girls, including girls sent
merely for education or rearing, are not to be admitted to the monastery.[38] Nuns may not even receive mail without the knowledge of the
abbess, and the abbess herself must meet visitors only in the company
of two or three other sisters.[39]

Caesarius's innovative *Rule for Nuns* appears to have had limited influence and to have fallen into disuse shortly after his death.[40] Nevertheless, along with centuries of local legislation, it found its way into
the store of documents that made up church tradition on female enclosure. Boniface VIII would probably have had access to this information, and although some elements of a rule drawn up in the sixth
century would have had little relevance for a pope living at the close
of the thirteenth, other principles could, and did, resonate. Although
Boniface VIII was not motivated to establish strict enclosure in order
to protect nuns from the random attacks and rapes common in Caesarius's time, he surely shared the bishop of Arles' desire to safeguard
nuns from themselves; to diminish, if not completely remove, worldly
temptations, so that in the words of *Periculoso:* "the nuns be able to
serve God more freely, wholly separated from the public and worldly
gaze and, occasions for lasciviousness having been removed, may most
diligently safeguard their hearts and bodies in complete chastity."

36. Ibid., 62.   37. Ibid., chap. 36, 182–83.
38. Ibid., chap. 7, 173; chap. 37, 183.
39. Ibid., chap. 38, 183; chap. 54, 189.
40. Cain, "Cloister," 255.

The same emphasis on female vulnerability is found in a letter of direction for the nuns of the Paraclete, written by the ill-fated philosopher and theologian Peter Abelard (1079–1142).[41] "Solitude," he warns the abbess, Heloise, "is indeed all the more necessary for your woman's frailty, inasmuch as for our part we are less attacked by the conflicts of carnal temptations and less likely to stray towards bodily things through the senses."[42] Paraphrasing the Rule of St. Benedict, Abelard goes on to say that the monastery should contain within its walls the necessities of everyday life, such as a garden, water, a mill and bakehouse, and places where the sisters could perform their daily tasks, so that no occasion be furnished for straying outside. In words that nearly duplicate those of *Periculoso,* he holds the local ordinary responsible for insuring that cloister regulations be maintained so that the nuns "preserve their bodies from carnal contagion."[43] Resembling a *florilegium* of biblical and patristic opinion more than a *regula* of the sort written by Caesarius, Abelard's proposed rule contains few practical details regarding enclosure of nuns.

Closer in time and frame of reference to *Periculoso* are the regulations formulated to govern two influential new orders of nuns, the Cistercians and the Poor Clares. Outgrowths of the vibrant spirituality of the twelfth and early thirteenth centuries, both of these communities possessed strict enclosure rules that have been viewed as directly influencing the genesis of *Periculoso.*[44]

41. *The Letters of Abelard and Heloise,* ed. and trans. Betty Radice, epistle 7.
42. Ibid., 196.   43. Ibid., 213.
44. Both Huyghe, *La clôture,* and Fontette, *Les religieuses,* note the connection between Cistercian and Poor Clare cloister regulations and *Periculoso.* Huyghe deals at length with Cistercian cloister regulations, 74–87, and states that those of the Poor Clares "preparèrent en fait l'intervention du Siege Apostolique pour l'Eglise Universelle en même temps et au même titre que les couvents des autres Ordres, comme les monastères de Cisterciennes, de Benedictines ou de Dominicaines," 94; also see 99; Fontette sees the usefulness of exploring "la genèse de la bulle [sic] *Periculoso* dans la législation sur la clôture des cisterciennes ou des clarisses," 11. She later adds: "On a même pu dire qu'elle [Cistercian cloister regulation] avait été l'inspiratrice de la bulle [sic] *Periculoso* de Boniface VIII, aboutissement de toutes les recherches des siècles précédents," 59–60. I will refer shortly to her comments on the Poor Clares, whom she sees as especially significant in influencing the development of *Periculoso.* Note that

In 1213, after virtually ignoring the existence of would-be Cistercian nuns for nearly a hundred years, the General Chapter of the order issued a statute designed to regulate observance in affiliated houses.[45] It declared that nuns already belonging to the order should not set foot outside convent walls without permission from their ultimate superior, the father abbot, and that in future no convents should be admitted unless fully cloistered. Out of all the possible conditions that might have been placed on convents desiring incorporation, this statute emphasized only strict enclosure. In 1218, the Chapter elaborated on its enclosure policy, stating that the abbess of a Cistercian house, accompanied by two nuns, might leave the monastery if necessary in order to transact the business of the house, but that even then consent of the father abbot should be secured if possible.[46]

In subsequent years Cistercian statutes show a concerted effort to

---

there were several earlier new orders of nuns, such as the Norbertines, Gilbertines, and the nuns of Fontevrault, whose cloister regulations might have directly affected later papal initiatives; see for instance, Huyghe, *La clôture,* 59–71; Fontette, *Les religieuses,* 16–24 and 65–80; Lawrence, *Medieval Monasticism,* 176–86. Coeval Dominican regulations for nuns (Gregory IX approved their rule on October 23, 1232), as Fontette notes above, might have also been influential. I have focused exclusively on the Poor Clares and Cistercians however, for two reasons. First, unlike some of the smaller early orders, such as the Norbertines, both Cistercians and Poor Clares proved resilient. They had European-wide appeal and consequently their rules were widespread— Huyghe, *La clôture,* 99. Second, the documentation of cloister regulations that exists for these two orders is legal and precise, making it particularly useful in the search for legislative forerunners to *Periculoso.* Huyghe, *La clôture,* 87, makes a point of distinguishing between the sort of documentation bequeathed by communities like Cluny and the much more technical Cistercian statutes.

45. *Statuta Capitulorum Generalium Ordinis Cisterciensis,* ed. J. M. Canivez, 8 vols. (Louvain, 1933–41) vol. 1, no. 3, 405 (1213) as cited in Huyghe, *La clôture,* 81 and 78; Lekai, *Cistercian Life and Culture,* 349; Lawrence, *Medieval Monasticism,* 185; McDonnell, *The Beguines,* 117. Nuns had been modeling their observance on the customs of Cîteaux since 1125 (the foundation of Tart) but had been excluded from the official structure of the order. The first reference of any kind to nuns appears in the statutes of the General Chapter in 1191—at which time the Chapter disavowed having jurisdiction over nuns. See Lekai, *Cistercian Life and Culture,* 347–49, and Huyghe, *La clôture,* 75–76.

46. Canivez, *Statuta* vol. 1, no. 84, 502 (1218) as cited in McDonnell, *The Beguines,* 117 and Huyghe, *La clôture,* 81.

enforce cloister rules in affiliated houses, to remove obstacles preventing the realization of strict enclosure, and to restrict even necessary excursions by the nuns. As Caesarius of Arles had recognized hundreds of years earlier, strict enclosure required the firm bedrock of economic self-sufficiency, and the Cistercian legislators in General Chapter began to address this practical necessity. A limit was set on the number of nuns allowed in each Cistercian community (a number above which the community might be reduced to "the disgrace of mendicancy"), and small houses within the same locality were required to merge.[47] *Conversi* or lay brothers were to provide the permanent revenues of each monastery via agricultural work and to see to the temporal affairs of a house.[48] Education of children within the cloister was discontinued; lay visitors, with the standard exception of nobility, were strictly limited.[49]

The papacy, it should be noted, assisted the order in its quest for absolute enclosure of its nuns. In 1234 Gregory IX issued a bull exempting several Cistercian abbesses from responding to legal citations that would require court appearances more than two days' journey from their monasteries.[50] In 1267, Clement IV ordered that the number of religious in each Cistercian house be fixed and limited—a ruling that aided Chapter efforts to set limits within the rapidly growing communities of women.[51]

The Cistercian insistence on strict enclosure of its incorporated female houses resulted in a drain of energy and such a substantial commitment of resources that the drastic legislation of 1228 seemed warranted. In that year the General Chapter issued a statute that completely barred existing convents from admission to the order and decreed that no new monastery of nuns could be built under Cistercian jurisdiction. If communities of nuns wished to take up the Cistercian rule, they would henceforth do so without official affiliation and with-

---

47. Cain, "Cloister," 263; Huyghe, *La clôture*, 83; see W. C. Jordan, "The Cistercian Nunnery of La Cour Notre-Dame de Michery—A House That Failed," 311–20, for evidence that even the best efforts of legislators sometimes failed to secure this most important objective: economic security of a cloistered community.

48. Huyghe, *La clôture*, 85.   49. Ibid., 80.
50. Ibid., 82.   51. Ibid., 84.

out supervision or spiritual direction.[52] A subsequent statute, issued the same year, made the General Chapter's policy of strict enclosure for the remaining Cistercian convents clear. All nunneries that belonged to the Cistercian order for seven years or more were to be completely enclosed within three years; those that refused such strict cloistering were to be summarily expelled.[53] Henceforth, strict enclosure was the requirement for any monastery of nuns claiming full Cistercian status.

Equal to, or perhaps surpassing, the Cistercian legislation in its significance for *Periculoso* is the rule granted to the Poor Clares by the 1264 bull of Urban IV, *Beata Clara*.[54] It was not, to be sure, the first set of regulations imposed upon the Poor Clares. Beginning with the terse *formula vitae* given the nuns by St. Francis, Clare and her followers re-

52. Canivez, *Statuta* vol. 2, no. 16, 68 (1228) as quoted in McDonnell, *The Beguines*, 118. The Latin reads: "Nulla monasteria monialium de cetero sub nomine aut sub jurisdictione Ordinis nostri construantur, vel Ordini socientur. Si quod vero monasterium monialium nondum Ordini sociatum vel etiam construendum, nostras institutiones voluerit aemulari, non prohibemus; sed curam animarum earum non recipiemus, nec visitationis officium eis impendemus."

53. Canivez, *Statuta* vol. 2, no. 17, 68–69 (1228) as quoted in McDonnell, *The Beguines*, 119. The Latin reads: "De his quae sunt iam Ordini sociatae a septem annis et infra, antiqua sententia teneatur, videlicet ut penitus infra triennium includantur; et quae includi noluerint, ubicumque fuerint, a custodia Ordinis se noverint separatas." Despite penalties imposed upon abbots who failed to respect this ruling, new foundations were, reluctantly, made at the request of popes and nobility, Sally Thompson, "The Problem of the Cistercian Nuns in the Twelfth and Early Thirteenth Centuries," in *Medieval Women*, ed. Derek Baker, 227–52, esp. 241.

54. *Bullarium Romanum* vol. 3, 709–21 (Potthast #18953). Cain, "Cloister," 266 says, "The key document for the nuns of St. Clare was the Bull *Beata clara*, of Urban IV in 1264. . . . The preciseness of this document aptly displays how legislators benefited from the labors of their predecessors and itself serves as a model of forthcoming papal pronouncements." Special significance is attributed to all the Poor Clare legislation by both Huyghe, *La clôture*, 94, and Fontette, *Les religieuses*, 11 and 60 n. 28: "A vrai dire, on attribue cette glorieuse paternité [of *Periculoso*] a plusieurs ordres féminins . . . cf. ce que nous dirons des clarisses." Sr. Chiara Augusta Lainati, "La clôture de Sainte Claire et des premières Clarisses dans la législation canonique et dans la pratique," 223–50, says: "La Pape Boniface, en effet, en donnant cette année-la [1298] les préscriptions générales sur la clôture monastique, ne faisait qu'étendre à toutes les moniales ce que les clarisses seules observaient déjà depuis 1219" (referring to the already rigid norms set down in the rule of Cardinal Hugolino), 223–24.

ceived, and sometimes rejected, rules of varying length and merit—
two of which were composed by cardinal protectors of the order: Hugolino (Gregory IX) in 1219 and Rainaldo (Alexander IV) in 1252.[55]
Each new rule tried to resolve, or to get rid of, the issue of corporate
as well as individual poverty—a "privilege" that St. Clare was not
prepared to renounce, even at the behest of a pope.[56]

While St. Clare waged a decades-long struggle for a rule that would
confirm the privilege of poverty, she clearly accepted the life of the
cloistered contemplative—in every version of the rule, including the
one formulated by Clare herself in 1253, strict enclosure remained a
constant.[57] In *Beata Clara* then, we see not only Urban IV's attempt to
impose uniformity of observance, but also a series of detailed cloister
regulations built upon decades of similar legislation.[58]

The relative importance of enclosure for the Poor Clares can be
gauged by the fact that it is mentioned in the very first of the rule's
twenty-six chapters. All who entered the order were to vow observance of the discipline of the rule "living in obedience, without property, and in chastity, under enclosure."[59] Enclosure, according to the
stipulations of the next chapter, was to be absolute and perpetual.
Nuns were to remain within their cloister for life and unauthorized
exit was permitted only when "dangerous necessity" such as fire or
hostile attack made it impossible to gain the required permission.[60]

55. See Rosalind and Christopher Brooke, "St. Clare," in *Medieval Women*,
ed. Derek Baker, 275–87; Fontette, *Les religieuses*, 129–51; Lainati, "La clôture
de Saint Claire," 223–50.

56. As Rosalind and Christopher Brooke note in "St. Clare," 284, the fact
that the Fourth Lateran Council of 1215 suspended the foundation of new orders inhibited action on a rule that included the novelty of total poverty.

57. Lainati, "La clôture de Sainte Claire," 223–24 and 247–50; Cain,
"Cloister," 266; R. and C. Brooke, "St. Clare," 287.

58. Fontette, *Les religieuses*, 151, says that Urban IV's rule was accepted by
the majority of Poor Clare monasteries in the fourteenth century.

59. *Bullarium Romanun* vol.3 *Beata Clara* c.1 710 ". . . vivendo in obedientia,
sine proprio, et in castitate, sub clausura." Worded in this way the Poor Clare
vows add a fourth, enclosure, to the traditional poverty, chastity and obedience.
The integral relationship established between the vows of chastity and enclosure will be elaborated upon by later (post-Trent) writers on the cloister of nuns
such as the Jesuit theologian and canonist Thomas Sanchez (d. 1610).

60. Ibid. c.2 p.710 "Omni namque tempore vitae suae hanc vitam profi-

This permission, in turn, could be granted only by the cardinal protector of the order, named by the pope—a designation of ordinary jurisdiction that established the Poor Clares as the first order to be bound by cloister regulations imposed and monitored by the papacy.[61] A few female servants, the chapter concludes, might be received into each house. They were to observe all the obligations of profession save for cloister regulations, since these sisters, with the license of the abbess, were permitted to leave the monastery on convent business.[62]

Chapters thirteen through eighteen of the rule deal in minute detail with the precautions to be taken to insure the observance of passive as well as active enclosure within each monastery—the material or physical aspects of enclosure. There is to be only one interior door or grille; it is to be entrusted to the custody of a nun of maturity and discretion. She should keep one of the two keys to this door (which is fortified with iron bars and almost always locked), the other being held by the abbess.[63] The exterior door is to be equally well guarded and locked, and a black woolen curtain is to be placed next to it on the

tentes, clausae manere firmiter teneantur infra murorum ambitum et intrinsecam clausuram monasterii deputatum, nisi forsan (quod absit) superveniret inevitabilis et periculosa necessitas, sicut exustionis ignis, vel incursus hostilis, seu alicuius huiusmodi, quae dilationem nullo caperet modo, ad egrediendi licentiam postulandam.''

61. Ibid. ''. . . nulla eis conceditur licentia vel facultas extra predictam clausuram ulterius exeundi, nisi forte de mandato aut auctoritate cardinalis Romanae Ecclesiae, cui a Sede Apostolica generaliter fuerit iste ordo commissus . . .'' See Peter Anson, ''Papal Enclosure for Nuns,'' 109–23, for the modern canonical distinction, traced back to this medieval precedent, between papal and episcopal enclosure. Papal enclosure currently refers to that imposed on all cloistered regulars who take solemn vows; episcopal enclosure affects only those who have taken simple vows.

62. Ibid. c.2, p.711 ''Possint autem in singulis monasteriis recipi aliquae, licet paucae, sub servitialium nomine, vel sororum, ad huiusmodi observantiam professionis astringendae, praeterquam ad articulum de clausura; quae de mandato vel licentia abbatissae interdum poterunt egredi ad negotia monasterii procuranda.''

63. Ibid. c.13, pp.714–15 ''Ad praedictum autem ostium custodiendum, aliqua talis ex sororibus deputetur, quae Deum timeat, sit matura moribus, sit diligens ac discreta, sitque convenientis aetatis,quae unam ipsius ostii clavem sic diligenter custodiat, ut numquam ea vel eius socia ignorante, ostium aliquando valeat aperiri. Reliquam vero clavem diversam ab illa custodiat abbatissa.''

interior, to insure that on the rare occasions on which the nuns, with permission of the abbess, should converse with any outsider they neither see, nor are seen by, their interlocutor.[64] Permission for any person, regardless of religious status or secular dignity, to enter the monastery must be obtained from the Apostolic See, or the cardinal protector—exceptions being made for a physician, in the event of grave illness, and then ónly with two companions from the *"familia"* of the monastery.[65] No extern may eat or sleep within the monastery, save with permission of the cardinal protector.[66] Cloister, in sum, complete and permanent, passive as well as active, is to be rigidly upheld by means of physical constraints as well as spiritual sanctions.

Periculoso thus appears to have been modeled largely on monastic regulations for the major religious houses of the time, in particular, the General Chapter rulings of the Cistercians and the rule granted to the Poor Clares by Urban IV. With significant omissions, such as any mention of the material aspects of enclosure so elaborately detailed for the Poor Clares, Boniface VIII drew on a considerable body of monastic legislation of recent vintage and with deep historical roots.

Another most interesting legislative forerunner with possible connections to *Periculoso* is a legatine decree issued for England in the mid-thirteenth century. From 1266 to 1268 Benedict Gaetani, the future Pope Boniface VIII, was in the service of the cardinal legate to England, Ottobuono.[67] If Ottobuono's actions during his brief papacy (as Pope Hadrian V, July 11–August 18, 1276) signify—he gave his erstwhile staff member supervision of the collection of papal tenths in France—

64. Ibid. c.16, p.716 "Cui pannus niger laneus interius taliter apponatur, quod nec sorores videre extra valeant, nec videri."

65. Ibid. c.18, p. 716 "De ingressu personarum in monsterium firmiter ac directe praecipimus ut nulla umquam abbatissa, vel eius sorores, aliquam personam religiosam, seu saecularem, aut cuiuslibet dignitatis in monasterii clausuram intrinsecam intrare permittant, nec omnino liceat alicui, nisi quibus concessu a Sede Apostolica fuerit, vel a cardinale cui fuerit sororum Ordo commissus: excipiuntur autem a dicta ingrediendi lege medicus, causa multum gravis infirmatis, et minutor, cum necessitas exegerit, qui non absque duobus sociis de familia monasterii introducantur. . . ."

66. Ibid. c.18, p.717 "Nulla autem personae extraneae intra monasterii clausuram liceat comedere vel dormire."

67. Boase, *Boniface VIII,* 11–13.

Gaetani worked well with, admired, and learned from the cardinal legate.[68] Zealous in the interests of reform, Ottobuono issued several decrees during his term as legate, one of which was aimed at the establishment of strict enclosure of all nuns in England. Promulgated under the rubric *Quod moniales certa loca non exeant,* this decree was canon 52 of the Legatine Council of St. Paul's London, April 1268; it was subsequently commented on by the influential canonist John Acton.[69]

Ottobuono stated that, having renounced the world for the perpetual service of Christ, nuns should preserve their innocence of mind and body by staying perpetually within the confines of their monasteries. Cloister precincts were to be strictly off limits to seculars, save only infrequently and for just cause. Nuns were not to speak to anyone, religious or secular, except in public, with at least one other nun present. Nuns were not to eat their meals outside of the monastery, save with permission of their superiors and then only when in the company of some relative or a person completely above suspicion. All places not specified above were forbidden to nuns, with the exception of the infirmary or other place to which an ailing nun might, with permission of her abbess, be sent for her health. Obedientiaries alone were to go outside on the business of the house, suitably accompanied, and even abbesses and prioresses were not to leave the monastery save for urgent necessity or evident advantage. Licenses to leave—predicated upon just or necessary cause and suitable companionship—were to be granted only sparingly. Archbishops, bishops, and other prelates with jurisdiction over communities of nuns were, Ottobuono concluded, to cause his statutes to be strictly observed.

As with the previously mentioned legislation of the Cistercians and Poor Clares, canon 52 can be seen as an important antecedent to *Periculoso,* because its content so clearly establishes contemporary eccle-

68. Ibid., 14. If in fact there were "English prejudices in Boniface's later deep distrust of France," they might have been learned during his association with Ottobuono.

69. For details of the council and the text of the statute see: *Councils and Synods,* ed. F. M. Powicke and C. R. Cheney, part 2, 738–39, 789–91. See chap. 7 for a more detailed summary of this canon and for the gloss of John Acton. See also Power, *Medieval Nunneries,* 346–47.

siastical concern for the establishment and maintenance of the cloister
for nuns. But it is the wording of Ottobuono's canon, not just the spirit,
that seems particularly significant in this instance. Echoes of *Quod
moniales* can be heard throughout Boniface VIII's constitution: Nuns
should not leave their monasteries, states Ottobuono, "so that they may
preserve the innocence of their hearts and bodies for the Lord." (*Periculoso* declares that cloister rules should enable "nuns to serve God
more freely, wholly separated from the public and worldly gaze and
that occasions for lasciviousness having been removed, they may most
diligently safeguard their hearts and bodies in complete chastity.")[70]
Canon 52 declares that "save for necessary and just cause, and then
only rarely, seculars are not to enter the monastery." (*Periculoso* requires
that " persons in any way disreputable, or even respectable shall not
be allowed to enter or leave [the monastery] unless a reasonable and
obvious cause exists . . .")[71] Ottobuono says that abbesses "shall not
leave their monasteries save for evident need of the monastery or out
of urgent necessity, and then [only] in respectable company." (*Periculoso* allows an abbess to leave to perform homage or fealty but only
"in respectable and decent company.")[72] Finally, Ottobuono charges
his ordinaries, "archbishops, bishops and other prelates of the church
upon whom the burden of visitation falls by law or custom, to cause
this statute to be strictly observed in the monasteries that they visit,
by virtue of holy obedience and under threat of divine judgement."
(Boniface VIII concludes with a similarly stern injunction: "We strictly

70. The Latin for canon 52 reads: ". . . eas exire non convenit, ut possint
domino cordis et corporis innocentiam conservare," *Councils and Synods,* 789;
for *Periculoso*: ". . . ut sic a publicis et mundanis conspectibus separatae omnino
servire Deo valeant liberius, et lasciviendi opportunitate sublata eidem corda
sua et corpora in omni sanctimonia diligentius custodire," *Appendix I.*
71. Canon 52: ". . . ut ad ea non nisi ex necessaria et justa causa persone
seculares accedant, et hoc non frequenter set raro," *Councils and Synods,* 790.
Periculoso: "nullique aliquatenus inhonestae personae nec etiam honestae (nisi
rationabilis et manifesta causa existat) . . . ingressus vel accessus pateat ad easdem," *Appendix I.*
72. Canon 52: "monasteria non exeant nisi ex evidenti monasterii utilitate
seu necessitate urgente, et cum honesta societate," *Councils and Synods,* 791.
Periculoso: "de monasterio cum honesta et decenti societate exire poterit eo casu
licenter," *Appendix I.*

enjoin patriarchs, primates, archbishops, and all bishops by virtue of
holy obedience, under threat of divine judgment and the prospect of
eternal damnation, that they take very diligent care that the nuns of
any monasteries within their city or diocese subject to them by law as
ordinaries and indeed even those that are immediately subject solely
to the authority of the Roman church and apostolic see . . . be enclosed
as soon as they can properly provide for this.")[73]

Whether they were nuns in recognized communities, orthodox but
"unruly" lay women, or heretical tertiaries, religiously active women
appear to have concerned Boniface VIII. In all of his legislation addressing religious women, but especially in the decree *Periculoso,* the
pope displayed genuine antipathy to untraditional female behavior, especially to wandering and preaching. The evidence suggests that this
aversion was not just the indulgence of a personal preference, nor
merely the articulation of conventional wisdom, but rather a response
to real challenges to his own authority and to that of the hierarchy at
large—challenges, moreover, that were not remote but that were nur-
tured, if not bred, in Italy itself, and that may have occasioned his stern
remedy. Strict enclosure, the absolute (and therefore novel) observance of an ancient and revered ideal, was the pope's prescription for
maintaining discipline among religious women who sought the highest palm that Christianity could offer them: recognized religious status
within a monastic community.

73. Canon 52: "Nichilominus archiepiscopis, episcopis, et aliis ecclesiarum prelatis quibus visitandi officium de iure seu consuetudine competit, in
virtute sancte obedientie et sub obtestatione divini iudicii districte precipimus
ut, monasteria monialium cum expedit visitantes, que statuta sunt firmiter faciant observari," *Councils and Synods,* 791. *Periculoso:* ". . . patriarchis, primatibus, archiepiscopis et episcopis universis districte in virtute santae obedientiae
sub obtestatione divini iudicii et interminatione maledictionis aeternae praecipiendo mandamus, quatenus eorum quilibet in civitate ac dioecesi propria in
monasteriis monialium sibi ordinario iure subiectis sua, in iis vero que ad Romanam immediate spectant ecclesiam sedis apostolicae auctoritate, abbates
vero et alii tam exempti quam non exempti prelati ecclesiarum, monasteriorum, et ordinum quorumcunque in monasteriis huismodi sibi subiectis, de
clausura convenienti, ubi non est, ipsorum monasteriorum expensis et fidelium
eleemosynis, quas ad hoc procurent, diligentius facienda, et de ipsis monialibus
includendis quam primum commode poterunt providere procurent, si divinae
ac nostrae indignationis voluerint acrimoniam evitare . . ." *Appendix I.*

Inspiration for, and in some cases the actual wording of, the majority of the clauses in *Periculoso* can be found in one or another piece of church legislation that preceded it. Whether one looks at Boniface VIII's insistence on active as well as passive enclosure, the limits he places on the number of nuns a monastery might accommodate, or his restriction of the travels of an abbess, churchmen at least as far back as Caesarius provided models for his rulings. Nor was Boniface the first pope to legislate on the subject of enclosure of nuns. As we have seen, Gregory IX and Clement IV buttressed the efforts of the Cistercians to achieve the strict enclosure of their nuns. For over forty years popes as enmeshed in worldly politics as Innocent III had found time to involve themselves actively in the issue of cloistering as it affected the Poor Clares.[74] Nevertheless, *Periculoso* continues to merit attention as a unique, and indeed original, piece of legislation.

Even when establishing the principle of papal enclosure in the case of the Poor Clares, Boniface VIII's predecessors were responding to the requests of religious rather than taking initiative. Before 1298 (and indeed again after that date, up to the time of the Council of Trent), that initiative generally came from monastic superiors acting on behalf of their orders.[75] Popes responded with exemptions, bulls, or licenses granted to particular orders on the basis of specific requests—requests often documented as such in the papal registers. In contrast, *Periculoso* laid down rules intended to apply to the whole of Christendom and designed to encompass all authorized orders of nuns. It strove to

74. Other examples of papal intervention preceding Boniface VIII, in support of efforts to enclose particular religious houses include the letter of 1222 written by Honorius III to the bishop of Bourges authorizing him to impose cloister on nuns "quae frequenter per vicos et plateas incedunt," Huyghe, *La clôture*, 96. Also, in 1273 Gregory X responded to a petition by the Priory of Carrow, forbidding them to receive more nuns into their monastery than they could adequately sustain—requests from English nobility had dangerously increased their numbers. Power, *Medieval English Nunneries*, 212. Note that neither of these letters is registered in Potthast.

75. Huyghe, *La clôture*, 58 says: "Bref, pendant toute cette période qui commence au XI siècle, à l'expansion clunisienne et qui va s'étendre jusqu'au Councile de Trente, la législation de la clôture n'est plus ni épiscopale ni conciliaire, sauf quelques rares exceptions: elle est d'origine regulière." *Periculoso* was, it seems, one of those "rare exceptions."

achieve uniformity of observance across national as well as local boundaries; its mechanisms for enforcement were in keeping with those pan-European pretensions. Whereas previous cloister regulation—the Poor Clares excepted—had depended on the abbot or, less frequently, the episcopal visitor, *Periculoso* required uniform hierarchical oversight, not respecting a monastery's exempt status, and it relied, if necessary, on the secular arm.

Periculoso was original, not in its specifics, but in its sweeping scope. Given the prestige of its author, the significance of the *Liber Sextus,* the legal compilation in which it appeared, and its purported range, *Periculoso* was pregnant with potential. That potential of course could be realized only to the extent that contemporaries—both those whose chief concern was interpreting the law and those charged with carrying it out—received, recognized, and fostered it.

T H R E E

Promulgation and Transmission of *Periculoso*

The publication of the *Liber Sextus* was an important event for European-wide Church administration, since the *Liber* encompassed nearly sixty-four years of papal and conciliar legislation.[1] As Pope Boniface explained in his 1298 bull of promulgation, the collection was designed to bring Gregory IX's five books to a state of perfection symbolized by the perfect number six.[2] Any papal decree included in the codification, regardless of its original scope, would henceforth be universally binding. The *Liber Sextus* appears, furthermore, to have found almost immediate favor among the academic lawyers to whom it was dispatched. Authorized copies were sent to the

1. On the *Liber Sextus* generally, see: Clarence Smith, *Medieval Law Teachers and Writers*, p. 57; A. Van Hove, *Prolegomena*, pp. 363–65; Alfons M. Stickler, *Historia iuris canonici latini*, pp. 257–64; J. F. von Schulte, *Geschichte der Quellen und Literatur des canonischen Rechts von Gratian bis auf die Gegenwart*, vol. 2, pp. 34–44; *NCE* vol. 8, p. 696.

2. The Latin text is printed in *Corpus Iuris Canonici* ed. Emil Friedberg, vol. 2, pp. 933–36. See Appendix I for my translation. The three canonists mentioned by Boniface VIII were indeed competent. Richard of Siena was a doctor of both laws, William of Mandegout was a diplomat and notary as well as a canonist, and Berengar Fredol, bishop of Béziers, was an ambassador to France and a lawyer (Boase, *Boniface VIII*, p. 92).

law schools of Padua, Rome, Salamanca, Toulouse, and Orleans, and comment on the *Sext* began soon after.[3]

At the same time that it was being circulated as part of the *Liber Sextus*, however, *Periculoso* was independently being transmitted to local ordinaries across Christendom.[4] Not surprisingly, given the initiatives discussed in the previous chapter, it makes a very early appearance in the enactments of the Cistercian General Chapter. In 1298 a statute reminded abbesses and nuns that all departures from their monasteries were formally forbidden, and that they were to keep their numbers within recognized limits to avoid falling into penury, "just as the Lord Pope fully ordained and decreed in this constitution."[5] The following

3. Boase, *Boniface VIII*, p. 93, notes that the universities "eagerly welcomed" the *Liber Sextus*.

4. Note that *Periculoso* does not appear to have had an independent existence before its publication in the *Liber Sextus*. It does not seem to have been a decretal letter, for instance. On the nature and form of decretal letters and the part that they have played since the twelfth century in enhancing the magisterial and judicial authority of the papacy, see especially: Charles Duggan, *Twelfth-Century Decretal Collections and Their Importance in English History*, pp. 19–23; Stephan Kuttner, "The Revival of Jurisprudence," in *Renaissance and Renewal in the Twelfth Century*, ed. R. Benson and G. Constable, pp. 316–19; for a discussion of the way in which academic canonists transformed individualized rescripts (decretals) into legal precedents that belonged to the general body of canon law, see: Steven Horwitz, "Magistri and Magisterium: Saint Raymond of Penyafort and the Gregoriana," pp. 211–14. Note also that scholarly works cite *Periculoso* variously: Power, p. 345, Schulenburg, p. 52, and Fontette, p. 61, call it a bull; LeClerq, p. 371, Le Bourgeois, p. 22, and Peter Anson, "Papal Enclosure for Nuns," p. 120, refer to it as a decretal; Huyghe calls it both a constitution and a decretal, while declaring "Nous ignorons les circonstances qui decidérent Boniface VIII à promulguer la Décrétale *Periculoso*" p. 99; Cain refers to it as a constitution and he too maintains: "The precise causes which motivated this papal pronouncement are not completely clear . . ." p. 267; *Periculoso* is classed as a constitution by the *DDC* vol. 3, p. 894, the *DTC* vol. 3, p. 252, and *The Catholic Encyclopedia*, vol. 4, p. 63.

5. Canivez, *Statuta* vol. 3 c. 2 p. 293 (1298) as cited in Huyghe, *La clôture*, p. 106. The Latin reads: ". . . super discursibus monialium Ordinis qui ipsius statum et clarum nomen multipliciter dehonestant, omnibus Abbatissis et monialibus Ordinis omnimodum egressa extra septa vel clausuram monasteriorum suorum omnino interdicit Capitulum Generale, necnon et receptionem personarum nisi quae de bonis seu proventibus ipsorum monasteriorum poterunt absque penuria sustentari prout Dominus Papa in sua constitutione plenarie sancivit et expressit."

year, the Chapter briefly reaffirmed its position, mandating that "the decree of our most holy father Pope Boniface VIII concerning the cloister be diligently observed."[6] The General Chapter of Chartreux also took the lead in incorporating *Periculoso* into its ordinances. Unlike the Cistercians, the Chartreux had not had an official policy prescribing enclosure of nuns before *Periculoso*. The statute of the chapter in 1298, then, formally introduced the cloister and linked the obligation directly to papal authorization.[7]

Although monastic superiors, often acting as local ordinaries, were among the first to receive *Periculoso*—many welcoming the *imprimatur* it placed on their own efforts to impose the cloister on the nuns within their orders—it was not only abbots and priors who had been entrusted with the enforcement of its universal enclosure regulations. *Periculoso* had specifically ordered bishops to oversee the establishment and observance of the cloister in all female monasteries under their jurisdiction, and, in this specific instance, to intervene in the ordering of exempt houses and houses under the direct jurisdiction of the papacy itself.[8] The execution of this expansive mandate required its diffusion to the provinces.[9]

Sometimes this process was couched in solemnity, at other times it

6. Canivez, *Statuta* vol. 3 c. 3, p. 294 (1299) as cited in Huyghe, *La clôture*, p. 106. The Latin reads: "Item diffusam prolixitatem definitionis anno praeterito editae de inclusione monialium Ordinis nostri et reformatione monasteriorum ipsarum, sic abbreviando declarat, Capitulum Generale quod statutum sanctissimi patris nostri Bonifacii Papae VIII super hoc editum diligentius observetur."

7. Huyghe, *La clôture*, p. 105; see also Fontette, *Les religieuses*, p. 87, and Cain, *Cloister*, p. 269. As Huyghe mentions, other monastic orders also promulgated statutes after *Periculoso* that explicitly referred to the decree. He goes so far as to say: "Désormais, toute la législation particulière ou générale de la clôture s'inspirera de la Décrétale *Periculoso*." Fontette, *Les religieuses*, p. 114, however, cites a clause from a 1312 Chapter meeting of Dominicans that treats of enclosure of nuns *without* reference to *Periculoso*.

8. See Appendix I for the text of *Periculoso*. Huyghe, *La clôture*, p. 104, elaborates on this paragraph, seeing in it Boniface VIII's genius for circumventing jurisdictional conflicts.

9. Boase, *Boniface VIII*, p. 93, says that *Periculoso* "seems to have been regarded more as a subject for legal study than for promulgation in provincial synods." Boase limited his study, however, to Boniface VIII's lifetime.

was rather informal. In 1300, English bishops meeting for the consecration of John Dalderby, bishop of Lincoln, had occasion for other business as well:[10] a memorandum from the meeting mentions almost incidentally that the assembled bishops agreed to enforce the enclosure of nuns as mandated by the recent papal constitution, *Periculoso*.[11] In contrast, the 1310 Provincial Council of Cologne formally promulgated *Periculoso* and in an accompanying injunction by Henry, archbishop of Cologne, detailed the "evils" it was designed to remedy:

> Nevertheless we often see that, having come out of their monasteries, [the nuns] wander about the roads and public places and frequent the houses of secular persons. And, what is more deplorable, having put off their religious habit, they appear in secular dress and bear themselves in public with so much vanity that their conduct may justly be considered suspicious, although their conscience be really pure and without sin. And although hitherto they have been menaced with divers penalties, nevertheless the more strictly they are forbidden to live after this fashion the more eagerly they disobey, so strongly do they hanker after forbidden things.[12]

Provincial synods of the fourteenth century usually assumed knowledge of *Periculoso* when they legislated about the enclosure of nuns, and they focused on strengthening the decree by exacting various penalties for violation.[13] The Council of Ravenna, held in 1317, published a summary of *Periculoso* in which it was noted that the constitution had been repeated and reinforced by local legislation.[14] In 1320, the Synod

10. *Councils and Synods* part 2, pp. 1204–5.

11. The Latin reads: "Consensum etiam extitit similiter quod ad clausuram monialium procederetur, prout dictus dominus archiepiscopus asservit se fecisse, precipue quia dictum fuit quod quidam erant in veniendo de curia Romana ad explorandum qualiter statutum de clausura predicta et alia per nunc papam edita fuerint observata." The archbishop mentioned is Winchelsey—see chap. 7 of this book for his efforts at enforcement of *Periculoso*.

12. Power, *Medieval Nunneries*, p. 360, note 1, translation hers.

13. See Cain, *Cloister*, pp. 269–70; Huyghe, *La clôture*, p. 105, as well as Cain, notes that a major weakness of *Periculoso* was its lack of sanctions—no firm penalty for illicit entry or exit from the cloister.

14. Mansi, vol. 25 c. 23, pp. 622–23; canon 23 also added needed speci-

of Perugia decreed that any cleric, religious, or layman who entered a convent of nuns, contrary to the constitution of the Lord Pope and without special license of the bishop, be excommunicated.[15] The Constitutions of Lucana, 1351, exacted the same penalty for unlicensed entrance into the cloister, with special exceptions for physicians attending a sick nun, masons, carpenters, those making essential deliveries and secular clerics brought in to hear confessions, anoint the sick, or bury the dead.[16] In extremely stern terms, canon 42 of the Council of Benevento (1378), classed violation of *Periculoso* with heresy, sodomy, perjury, incest, sacrilege, arson and infanticide, as crimes reserved to the bishop: only at the time of death could the delinquent be absolved from his sin by anyone other than the bishop.[17]

As late the Council of Mainz (1549), provincial ordinaries summoning synods continued to refer to *Periculoso* and to levy severe sanc-

---

ficity to *Periculoso,* more precisely defining "cloister" and reassuring those who, it seems, feared sin even in well-regulated conversation with the nuns. Precautions to be taken when speaking with nuns are reminiscent of those found in the rule of the Poor Clares: ". . . statuimus, quod nullus de caetero poenas in dictis constitutionibus contentas incurrat pro ingressu monasterii dummodo locum monialibus pro clausura deputatum per locorum ordinarios non ingrediantur, in quo casu firmae et illabatae dictae constitutiones permaneant. Concedimus etiam, quod quaelibet persona, quae non sit notabiliter suspecta, possit loqui monialibus memoratis, sine metu poenae, ad cratam [wickerwork] seu fenestram ferream, de licentia abbatissae, seu priorissae, vel ejus locum tenentis: praesentibus tamen semper duabus ex monialibus ab abbatissa vel priorissa, vel earum vice tenente, ut praemittitur specialiter deputatis, que semper videre possint et audire sororem, seu monialem, ad fenestram vocatam."

15. Mansi, vol. 25 c. 6, p. 641. The rubric reads: "Quod nullus clericus aut religiosus audeat intrare monasteria monialium nisi de licentia." Taking a hard line, canon 6 concludes: "nolumus etiam quod aliquis clericus aut religiosus ad loquendum eisdem sine licentia speciali."

16. Mansi, vol. 26 c. 56, p. 278. Canon 56 prescribes its penalty in no uncertain terms and reserves the right of absolution to the bishop save when death is imminent: "In omnes et singulos contrarium facientes praeter poenam libram X denarii lucensis, cujus quintam partem denuntianti volumus applicari ex nunc prout ex tunc excommunicationis sententiam ferimus in his scriptis. Item quod nullus facendos audiat confessiones earum, vel absolvere possit sine nostra licentia speciali vel illius, quem ad hoc duxerimus deputandum mortis articulo semper excepto."

17. Mansi, vol. 26 c. 42, pp. 640–42.

tions on violators of the decree; not so subsequent popes.[18] Clement V, Boniface VIII's immediate successor, appears to have had little interest in either reaffirming or elaborating upon *Periculoso* when he presided over the General Council of Vienne, 1311–12.[19] Unlike the general councils of Constance (1414–18) and Basel (1431–45), in which issues of schism and reunion eclipsed all discussion of monastic reform, several canons of the council of Vienne deal with monastic regulation; two, which were to become very well known, deal specifically with religious women.[20] Far from conflicting with the regulations laid down by Boniface VIII, the legislation sponsored by Clement V at Vienne was frequently cited by the canonists who glossed *Periculoso*.[21] Clement V's failure to mention Boniface VIII's decree surely had less to do with a difference of opinion about the proper conduct of nuns than with politics. Since he was largely subservient to the French king, Clement V could hardly have officially endorsed the work of Philip's former enemy.[22]

While there was considerable regional variation—a fact that the canonists noted well—*Periculoso* seems to have been published with some fanfare and sucessfully integrated into monastic and diocesan legislation, if not practice, throughout Europe. Dispatched to the major European law schools as part of the *Liber Sextus,* it became almost immediately an object of academic interest as well.

18. Mansi, vol. 32 c. 79, p. 1429; see also the Synod of Venice, 1433, Mansi, vol. 31, p. 349. Both are cited by Cain, *Cloister,* p. 270.

19. For background on the council and texts of all of its canons in Latin and English see: *Decrees of the Ecumenical Councils,* vol. 1, pp. 333–84.

20. I refer especially to canon 16 of the Council of Vienne, *Cum de quibusdam mulieribus,* which was incorporated into the *Clementines* 3.11.1 and popularized by the recent interest in the Beguines, the subject of Clement V's concern. Canon 15, *Attendentes,* dealt with convent discipline and was incorporated into the *Clementines* (3.10.2) as well. Canonists commenting on *Periculoso* frequently cite *Attendentes.* Note that after Vienne and prior to Trent, female monastic regulation simply did not feature in ecumenical council canons—refer again to Huyghe's observation, noted in chap. 2 note 72.

21. See chaps. 4–6 of this study for examples of this pattern of citation.

22. For details about Clement V's relations with Philip see Brian Tierney, *The Crisis of Church and State,* pp. 184 and 192. In a decree of April 1311, Clement V pronounced Philip's actions toward Boniface VIII "guiltless," saying that he and his had "acted out of an estimable, just and sincere zeal and from the fervor of their Catholic faith." Tierney, *Crisis,* p. 192.

F O U R

Earliest Commentators on *Periculoso*

The earliest period of comment, query, and analysis of *Periculoso* produced by continental jurists ends with the publication of the so-called *Glossa Ordinaria* of Joannes Andreae. As the name suggests, the ordinary gloss became a standard reference book for lawyers as well as a model for later commentators on the *Liber Sextus*. After Joannes Andreae, those canonists who chose the gloss as their vehicle for comment on *Periculoso* consistently copied the *Glossa Ordinaria*. Of course the canonists of the fourteenth century were already working within an established and rather rigid framework. The order in which a particular piece of decretal legislation would be commented on, the position of both text and comment, had been set long before—ever since the *Compilatio Prima* (1190) in fact.[1] After the publication of the ordinary gloss, both the choice of words to be glossed and the order in which they would be commented on also became standardized. Such standardization—a convenience for the working lawyer, but a measure that deprives the historian of any chance to speculate on a given author's motives for placing one text beside another—is all the more apparent when set next to the work of the two glossators who

1. See chap. 3, note 4 for details about decretal compilation.

predated Joannes Andreae. Although Joannes Monachus and Guido de Baysio produced commentary on *Periculoso* that was much briefer than that of Joannes Andreae, theirs were also freer in form. Their glosses show us what there was about *Periculoso* that immediately struck contemporary jurists as significant, and not what they felt compelled to include as part of a scholastic exercise.

The first commentary on *Periculoso* that survives is the *Apparatus super Decretalium* written by Jean Le Moine, also known as Joannes Monachus.[2] The work was completed rather quickly—it was sent to the University of Paris on the sixteenth of February 1301—yet as Joannes's biography suggests, he was well equipped to produce a commentary of some merit and one that would be frequently cited by contemporaries. In fact, his *Apparatus* actually became the standard gloss at Paris and other French schools of canon law, while Joannes Andrea's *Apparatus* was taught at Bologna and most other law schools as the *glossa ordinaria* on the *Liber Sextus.*

Born about 1250 in Crécy, in the Diocese of Amiens, Joannes Monachus studied philosophy and theology in Paris, where he became a canon. After receiving his doctorate in both canon and civil law, he spent some time in Rome, where he became an auditor of the Roman Rota and where he gained favor with Charles II, king of Naples. He was created a cardinal by Celestine V in 1294 and Boniface VIII named him papal legate to France in 1302. He negotiated unsuccessfully with the king of France over the terms of *Unam Sanctam,* and left Paris in 1303. In the last years of his life he became papal chancellor; he died at Avignon on August 22, 1313, and was buried in the chapel of the college that he had founded in Paris.

In his *Apparatus super Decretalium* Joannes employs a straightforward technique. Prefacing his discussion of each canon in the *Liber Sextus* with a summary of its principal points, he then proceeds to a

2. See: *DDC* vol. 6 p. 113 and Schulte, *QL* vol. 2 pp. 191–93, for details of his life and work. Existing in a large number of manuscripts, the *Apparatus super Decretalium* was first printed at Paris in 1535, under the title *Glossa Aurea.* This printed version, which contained lengthy additional commentary by a Parisian advocate named Philip Probus, was reissued in Venice in 1558 and 1602. I will be using the 1535 edition, repr. 1968, cited hereafter as *Glossa aurea.*

gloss of key words. His treatment of *Periculoso* is brief—it occupies one column in the sixteenth-century edition that I consulted—and follows his general scheme. After his summary of the principal provisions of *Periculoso* Joannes appends a question: How can any nun be bound to obey a rule of life stricter than the one under which she had entered the order?[3] It was a question with a hallowed tradition. Gratian had touched upon it in his *Decretum* when he asked whether a monk might transfer to a stricter order or impose upon himself rigors that his brethren were not obliged to share.[4] Gratian answered his own question by allowing such departures from the general customs of a monastic house, but only with the consent of the abbot/abbess. As subsequent commentary on the *Decretum* illustrated, not all canonists were willing to accept such a neat solution to a question that involved the essential tension between the demands of the law and those of the spirit, between canon and conscience. Indeed Rufinus, one of earliest Decretists, had argued that unless it could be proven that his motives were suspect, a monk might tranfer to a stricter monastery even if his abbot forbade him to do so![5]

3. *Glossa aurea* to *VI* 3.16.1 v.*clausura* "Sed quomodo aliqua artatur gravius quam inceperit ut ea invita vinculo graviori stringatur?" Note that the Latin for all canonical texts quoted directly, and for those drawn from sources that are not readily available will be reproduced in the footnotes. Repeated allegations, unless they are especially significant to my argument, will not be reprinted in the original.

4. *Decretum* C. 20 q. 4 especially *dicta post causa* 3; Gratian concluded that for the good of their souls monks and nuns might transfer to stricter monasteries, assume particular vows of abstinence, or inflict upon themselves other rigors that departed from the general custom of their houses; but that they could do so *only* with the consent of their abbot/abbess in order to avoid scandalizing their fellow religious.

5. See for instance the treatment of C. 20 q. 4 in the following: Rolandus, *Die Summa Magistri Rolandi*, ed. F. Thaner (Innsbruck, 1879); Rufinus, *Summa decretorum*, ed. H. Singer (Paderborn, 1922); *Summa Parisiensis on the Decretum Gratiani*, ed. T. McLaughlin (Toronto, 1952); and C. 88 in *Summa Elegantius in iure divino seu Coloniensis* vol. 1 Tom. III, ed. G. Fransen and S. Kuttner (Vatican City, 1986). The tension between conscience and canon, the need to preserve discipline while at the same time guarding against an authoritarianism that would make the law impervious to divine inspiration (what Pope Urban II had termed private law, or that law which is written in the heart by the inspiration of the Holy Spirit) was a continual theme in canonical literature. Thus Rufinus,

For Joannes Monachus, however, the troublesome problems surrounding the need to preserve discipline and at the same time recognize the importance of divine inspiration as manifested in the
individual conscience never emerge. He answers his own question by
merely denying that *Periculoso* constitutes anything like a reformation
of the existing rules of life for religious women. In spite of its strict
provisions, he contends, *Periculoso* actually adds nothing new to existing monastic rules for nuns but only addresses *the manner in which* those
rules should be lived out. No conflict arises between existing norms
and new ones, or between the letter and the spirit. It is just not fitting
for religious women to wander about, to cohabit, or in other ways associate, with men. *Periculoso* simply guarantees that these things will
not happen.[6] Joannes finds support for his ingenious solution not only
from canon law, e.g., Boniface VIII's stipulation that women not be
held to appear personally in courts of law, but also from an oblique
reference to the frailty and dependence of women in a Roman law concerning the property of minors and wards.[7]

---

one of Gratian's earliest glossators, felt that even more latitude was needed in
resolving the issue posed by C. 20 q. 4 : "By the authority of Pope Urban, and
resting upon the position of the master [Gratian], we say that a monk is able
to transfer to a stricter monastery even with the abbot contradicting, unless he
should wish to do this out of levity or cupidity or similar reason, and not for
the sake of leading a more severe life. If therefore those *capitula* [C.20 q.4 c.3]
say that an abbot should not accept any monk who does not have the consent
of his own abbot [to enter a different house], these words must always be sup-
plied: unless he should wish to transfer to a stricter monastery" (Singer,
p. 382).

6. "Solutio: hic nil ad regulam adiicitur sed modus in cohabitando taxatur
et secumdum naturam rei fit, cum non deceat mulieres evagari nec virorum
immisceri."

7. *VI* 2.1.2 The rubric reads: "Mulieres personaliter ad iudicium quaecum-
que causa, in iure non expressa, invitae trahendae non sunt." This allegation
will be treated in depth in the *Glossa Ordinaria; Codex* 5.51.13, is indeed an
oblique reference discussing the manner in which the property of a ward or a
minor ought to be inventoried. Note that Roman law texts are cited throughout
from the critical edition of the *Corpus iuris civilis,* ed. Paul Krueger, Theodor
Mommsen, Rudolf Schoell, and Wilhelm Kroll, 3 vols. (Berlin: Weidmann,
1872–95). Citations to the *Digest* also refer to *The Digest of Justinian,* Latin text
ed. Theodor Mommsen and Paul Krueger, English trans. ed. Alan Watson, 4
vols. (Philadelphia: University of Pennsylvania Press, 1985).

Since *Periculoso* allowed outsiders entrance to the confines of the cloister "for a reasonable and obvious cause" with the receipt of a special license, Joannes Monachus next asks: "Who may grant such a license?"[8] Relying on Gratian's discussion of monastic independence from the episcopacy, he concludes that the bishop is not automatically the one to grant such a right.[9] Abbesses, on the other hand, also cannot grant license to enter, since they themselves are bound by cloister regulations and therefore ought do nothing to abrogate them. The Roman law maxim that women frequently act to their own disadvantage is cited in support of this conclusion.[10] Thus, the only one who can grant a license to enter the cloister, according to Joannes, is the ordinary who has jurisdiction over both the nuns and their rule of life. Once again, Roman law is cited to bolster this conclusion: "He to whom legal jurisdiction is given is also held to be invested with all the powers necessary for its exercise."[11]

Turning to the practical matter of the economic solvency of a newly enclosed community of nuns, Joannes Monachus concurs with *Periculoso*'s stipulations limiting the number of nuns in each house. Religious women need these and other protections, he says, since they are not afforded the same liberty as their male counterparts. Religious men are permitted to have contact with society in order to acquire the necessities of life. Consequently, the provision which declares null and void the admission of any nun over and above the number that one community can provide for does not extend to monks.[12]

8. *Glossa aurea* to *VI* v.Episcopus "non, . . . Abbatissa non, quia artatur hac clausura, ergo contra eam non habet facere . . ."

9. He cites specifically: *Decretum* C. 18 q. 2 c. 1, 6, 21.

10. *Codex* 5.1.4 is cited. It presents the case of a deceased father's wishes concerning his daughter's marriage and concludes that his directives are not to be altered by compromises that the daughter might want to make with her guardian or curator, since "the majority of women are ever found to favor opinions contrary to their own best interests." Joannes precedes the citation with the words: "Et mulieres ut plerunque adversus sua commoda laborare nituntur."

11. *Digest* 2.1.2.; he also cites *X* 1.29.5 concerning the vested powers of judges delegate; the rubric reads: "Per simplicem commissionem causae potest delegatus citare, contumacem punire, et reliqua facere, quae spectant ad causam."

12. *Glossa aurea* to *VI* 3.16.1 v. *decernentes* "secus in masculis, quibus est

The remainder of the *Glossa aurea*'s treatment of *Periculoso* consists of little more than Romano-canonical citations in support of subsequent clauses in the decree. However, special mention is made of both papal means and might. Joannes defines "our wrath," the words Boniface had used to refer to his sanctions against noncompliance, as excommunication.[13] He also uses language clearly in accord with the ideals that Boniface VIII would soon articulate in *Unam Sanctam* when glossing the last two sentences of *Periculoso,* which deal with papal invocation of secular power to punish those who resist the decree: "For it is indeed proper that the power of the Church be supported by the secular arm, not to its prejudice but rather because such service is pleasing to God."[14] Joannes Monachus treats *Periculoso* much as we might expect a busy fourteenth-century canonist, who is also a cardinal, to do—with dispatch, no equivocation, and a heavy reliance on papal authority bolstered by references to the civil law.

A similar brevity, but with a narrower focus, characterizes the *Apparatus* of Guido de Baysio—the second surviving commentary on the *Liber Sextus,* written no later than 1302.[15] A Bolognese canonist noted less for his work on the *Liber Sextus* than for his *Rosarium* (rosegarland), which amplified the standard gloss on the *Decretum,* Guido's reputation for learning, like that of Joannes Monachus, created a demand for all his work. Born in Reggio nell'Emilia, where his parents were in political exile, Guido took his doctorate in canon law there in

---

permissum cetibus hominum immisceri, et acquirere vite necessaria, unde hic pinguis providetur mulieribus." The practical questions involved in applying cloister regulations to male as opposed to female communities surface again and again in canonical commentary and will be dealt with at the close of this chapter and in my conclusion.

13. *Glossa aurea* to *VI* 3.16.1 v.*acrimoniam* "vel dic acrimonia descendit ab acer et moneo, unde acrimonia, acris monitio, unde designat austeritatem in vultu." Joannes cites the *Codex* 1.2.5 which condemns the usurper of church property to perpetual exile after undergoing the punishment prescribed for sacrilege.

14. *Gloss aurea* to *VI* 3.16.1 v.*brachii* "hoc enim decet ut potestas ecclesiastica iuuetur per secularem, non ad preiudicandum, set potius ad ea que deo sunt placita prosequendum."

15. For details about Guido de Baysio's life as well as his work see: *DDC* vol. 5 p. 1008; Schulte, *QL* vol. 2 pp. 86–90.

1276. He taught first at Reggio and then at Bologna, and in 1296 Boniface VIII named him archdeacon of Bologna; hence he is most often cited by later writers as "the Archdeacon" rather than by name. He taught canon law privately until 1301, when the city of Bologna appointed him as Professor of Canon Law for three years. In 1304 he joined the papal court at Avignon, where Benedict XI named him a papal chaplain. He died in 1313.

Although Hain lists an edition printed in Milan in 1480, the *Apparatus* exists chiefly in manuscript. The space devoted to *Periculoso* in the fragment of the *Apparatus* that I have looked at is small—less than 200 words—but that terse paragraph is dense with allegations or proof texts.[16] It is those texts, in turn, that are the principal interest. Beginning with a definition of the word *periculoso*—that which is pernicious, detestable, execrable—Guido de Baysio takes pains to identify the virtues at risk when nuns wander: *modestia,* the consituent parts of which are fragility, shyness, and chastity, and *verecundia,* which is bashful modesty. Guido notes that it is this modesty of the female sex which is spoken of in the Old Testament description of the way in which Rebecca, when first catching sight of her future husband Isaac, hid her face with her veil.[17] He adds that in *Leviticus* the sons of Israel are warned to shun all uncleanliness *(immundicia),* and that *verecundia* is to be understood as the same sort of active avoidance of all impurity: a dread of contamination.[18]

Because the *Apparatus* singles out the special importance of modesty for women, it is surprising, at first glance, to find that when glossing the words *extra sua monasteria,* Guido uses supporting texts that refer solely to monks. Guido states that it is wicked to go outside of

16. I am indebted to Professor James A. Brundage for his transcription of Cambridge, Gonville and Caius College MS 493/262, fol.264 ra, henceforth cited as Guido de Baysio, *Apparatus.*

17. Guido de Baysio, *Apparatus* to *VI* 3.16.1 v.*modestia* "id est mansuetudine verecundia modestia partes sunt fragilitas, pudor, castitas. *Verecundia* id est pudore modestia de hac verecundia sexus feminini loquitur: Genesis 24:61 [as cited in] *Decretum* C. 30 q. 5 c. 8."

18. Ibid. "scriptum est vercundes vel veretites facite filios Israel ab omni immundicia. . . . [Leviticus 15:31] . . . et dic verecundos vel verentes, scilicet ut verecundia vel timore essent ab omni immundicia."

the confines of one's monastery, since following the Rule of St. Benedict monks ought to stay within the cloister precincts.[19] And he concludes his observations with the hoary caution that monks should be content to stay within the cloister, since a monk can no more live out of the monastery than a fish can survive out of water.[20]

In Guido de Baysio we have our first example of a canonist attempting to resolve the paradox of *Periculoso*. Working within a tradition that, as we have seen, stressed the theoretical equality of the vocations of monks and nuns, Guido was faced with a decree that mandated a starkly different style of life for nuns based on the fragility of the female sex. Joannes Monachus had used scholastic method, linguistic sleight of hand, to avoid confronting the anomalies of the Bonifacian legislation—*Periculoso* had not altered the rule of life for nuns, only the manner in which that rule should be lived out. Guido de Baysio chose instead to change the very terms of the discussion. Instead of acknowledging the novelty of *Periculoso* as law, Guido approached it as a moral precept, a counsel to perfection akin to that which St. Benedict had given to his monks. In this way Guido could catalogue the virtues peculiar to the female sex, and even emphasize the fragility of that sex—the observation of difference being clearly distinct from an acknowledgment of spiritual inferiority. At the same time, by supporting *Periculoso*'s demand for strict claustration of nuns with precepts of spiritual direction originally aimed at monks, he could preserve the essential equivalence of male and female religious vocations even as reality (and his own later comments as cited in Joannes Andreae's *Novella*) clearly contradicted it.

Within a very few years after the start of the new century, then, Joannes Monachus and Guido de Baysio had already addressed some of the chief questions and concerns raised by *Periculoso*. Joannes broached the issue of the potential conflict between the dictates of in-

19. Guido de Baysio, *Apparatus* to *VI* 3.16.1 v.*extra sua monasteria* "et hoc pessime, nam monachis secundum regulam sancti benedicti intra claustrum morari precipitur: *Decretum* C. 16 q. 1 c. 11."

20. Ibid. "monachus claustro suo sit [sic] contentus, quia sicut piscus sine aqua caret vita, ita monachus sine monasterio." This time-worn maxim surfaces again and again. Guido's citation for it is *Decretum* C. 16 q. 1 c. 8 attributed, perhaps erroneously, to "Pope Eugenius."

dividual conscience and monastic rule; he also paved the way for future discussions about the integrity of the monastic rule in the face of
papal prerogative directed at its reform. He raised the question of jurisdiction over monasteries—a topic that would live on in other commentary as well—and the practical problems of keeping a cloistered
monastery solvent. With implications for future commentary as well
as the late medieval papacy, he glossed the penalty attached to Boniface VIII's decree as excommunication. Joannes used terminology that
highlighted the differences between women and men, and he seemed
to be more than willing to see strict enclosure as necessitated by the
greater frailty of women, yet in essence he was interested in judicial
liabilities rather than the moral consequences of *Periculoso*. In contrast,
Guido de Baysio lingered over the spiritual consequences of an unregulated life for nuns, while still trying to preserve the ideal of a spiritual equivalence between monks and nuns. Both Joannes and Guido
de Baysio would have their admirers; they would both be cited regularly by a subsequent generation of canonists. Yet as important as these
writers were, their glosses were both soon supplanted by the monu-
mental work of Joannes Andreae.

One of Guido de Baysio's students, Joannes Andreae was born
about 1270 at Rifredo, near Florence, and moved with his family to
Bologna while he was still young.[21] He studied grammar at his father's
school and briefly studied theology under John of Parma and Roman
law under Martinus Syllimani and Richardus Malumbra. He took his
doctorate in canon law between 1296 and 1300 and was Professor of
Canon Law at Bologna by 1303. By 1305 Joannes Andreae had fin-
ished his *Apparatus* to the *Liber Sextus* (additions, always printed with
the *Apparatus,* were completed between 1334 and 1342). It was almost immediately accepted as the *Glossa Ordinaria* or standard gloss
on the text. He taught in Padua for a few years, but in 1320 returned
to Bologna, where he remained a professor of law until his death of
the plague in 1348. Joannes Andreae's wide learning, huge juristic
output, and tremendous popularity among contemporary canonists
are all the more notable since he was a layman—his *Novella,* an ad-

21. For biographical details see *DDC* vol. 6 pp. 89–91; Smith pp. 72–73;
Schulte *QL* vol. 2 pp. 205–29.

ditional commentary on the *Liber Sextus,* was named after his youngest daughter.

The *Glossa Ordinaria,* appended to nearly all of the early manuscripts and printed editions of the *Liber Sextus,* became the chief source of commentary for students of the law and set a pattern of citation that few subsequent commentators failed to follow.[22] It is a large work— nearly 400 pages in the printed edition I consulted—that draws on ancient as well as contemporary sources. Consequently, Joannes's treatment of *Periculoso* is longer than anything we have encountered so far. The relative importance that Joannes attached to *Periculoso* can be judged from the fact that he devoted two and a half pages to comment on it, while allotting only one to a gloss of *VI* 1.7.1 *de renunciatione*— the *capitulum* that dealt with the renunciation of the papacy, which was clearly an important position statement given the difficulties surrounding Boniface VIII's election.[23]

Joannes begins his comment on *Periculoso* with a brief summary of the constitution, dividing it into four parts: the statement of purpose and definition of enclosure for nuns; the prescription limiting the number of nuns within non-mendicant communities; provisions regarding the occasions when nuns might have to leave their cloisters; instructions to the executors of the decree. Bowing to his teacher, Guido de Baysio, Joannes adds that *Periculoso* was meant to provide a remedy for danger, "what the Archdeacon defines as pernicious, detestable, execrable."[24]

Glossing the next words, *laxatis habenis,* with a literal bent, Joannes draws the analogy between a religious woman who has "thrown off

22. I have collated three early editions of the *GO* (as listed in the bibliography) which are virtually identical. The few discrepancies that exist will be noted in the footnotes. The text used in the present analysis (Lyons, 1605) postdates the edition of the so-called *Correctores Romanae* .

23. See chapter 1 of this study for Boniface VIII's election difficulties.

24. *GO* to *VI* 3.16.1 v.*periculoso:* "ADDITIO. Et ut infra dicit glossa praemitte hic litteram illam, cupientes salubriter providere. Et Archidiaconus exponit periculoso, pernicioso, detestabili, execrabili." Note that in the 1605 edition the *GO* proper is preceded by a *casus* (written by one "Dom[inicus])" offering a detailed paraphrase of *Periculoso,* styled as a reply to the question posed by someone in the presence of Boniface VIII: "Most holy father I wish to be told in what state/condition nuns ought to live?"

the reins of nunnish modesty" and a horse that, casting off its reins, runs wherever it will.[25] Nor is he more imaginative when defining, by allegation, the nature of that "nunnish modesty." Citing the same quotation concerning the veiling of Rebecca that Guido de Baysio had used, Joannes adds an even more well-known allegation, attributed to St. Augustine, that explains the need for such symbols of modesty. Man alone, according to Augustine, was made in the image and likeness of God; consequently, as the apostle Paul states, men need not cover their heads, but women should be veiled since "they possess neither the glory nor the image of God."[26]

Commenting on the line in *Periculoso* in which Boniface VIII speaks of the admission of suspect persons into monasteries, "to the injury of those who *by free choice* vowed their chastity," Joannes remarks, not as one would expect, about the dangers of association with such persons, but instead (and perhaps in anticipation of his subsequent comments on the thorny issue of freedom of conscience among professed religious) about the notion that monastic vows are, and must be, taken of one's own volition.[27] He alleges Gratian's case of a young monk compelled by his father to enter a monastery, and the oblate's subsequent, and blameless, rejection of his unwonted burden.[28] He clarifies his argument with a second citation, attributed to Pope Clement III, that states that a daughter who was pledged to a monastery when she was under twelve years of age would be bound to remain in religion only if she freely accepted the veil when she reached maturity.[29]

When glossing the word *offensam*, which refers to the injury that associating with seculars might cause the chastity of women under vows of religion, Joannes Andreae cites a lengthy patristic admonition

25. *GO* to *VI* 3.16.1 v.*laxatis habenis* "similitudinarie ad equum, qui laxatis habenis currit quo vult."

26. *GO* to *VI* 3.16.1 v.*verecundia;* he cites *Decretum* C. 30 q.5 c.8, as had Guido de Baysio, and C. 33 q. 5 c. 13 for St. Augustine's reference to veiling of women: ". . . mulier ideo velat quia non est gloria aut imago Dei."

27. *GO* to *VI* 3.16.1 v.*spontanea* "Alias non obligarentur."

28. *Decretum* C. 20 q. 3 c. 4.

29. *X* 3.31.12 The rubric reads: "Si filia, minor XII annis a praentibus monasterio tradita, maior facta sponte veletur, ad saeculum redire non potest."

against corporeal corruption of women. Corporeal corruption of women, according to St. Cyprian, can come about not only through sexual intercourse, but through lewd caresses and kisses as well. All such activity is forbidden to the nun because of her vows, which are analogous to those taken in marriage. Expanding on the parallels between the heavenly spouse of the nun and a mortal husband, Cyprian concludes with a stern warning: if a husband who comes home to find his wife in the arms of another man is indignant, outraged, and even driven to pick up his sword, how much anger will Christ, the lord and judge, show toward a woman who, having vowed her virginity to him, defiles it![30]

Joannes next grapples with the difficult issue—one that had been neatly dismissed by Joannes Monachus—of the extent to which *Periculoso* imposes a rule of life on professed nuns that is stricter than the one under which they entered their orders. "But when may a stricter life be imposed on professed nuns?" he asks, and proceeds to adduce authorities for and against any imposition.[31] First he uses a citation from the *Decretum,* employed by Gratian in his discussion of whether virginity could be commanded: one should be persuaded to keep one's virginity, but not ordered to do so, since doing something because you promised it is of greater value than fulfilling a command.[32] The case of the unwilling oblate, mentioned above, also reappears to underscore the argument that no one can be compelled to advance spiritually. Finally, after mentioning Joannes Monachus's argument that *Periculoso* should be countenanced since it really adds nothing new to monastic rules, Joannes draws his own conclusion that is in some ways equally ingenious. All arguments adduced above, he says, apply to secular clerics but *not* to religious. Monks and nuns have relinquished their

30. *GO* to *VI* 3.16.1 v.*offensam;* he cites *Decretum* C 27 q 1 c 4 for the patristic text: ". . . Si superveniens maritus sponsam suam iacentem cum altero videat, nonne indignatur et fremit et per zeli dolorem, portat gladium in manu sua? Et Christus Dominus et iudex noster, cum virginem suam sibi dicatam et sanctitati suae destinatam iacere cum altero cernit, quam indignatur et irascitur?"

31. *GO* to *VI* 3.16.1 v.*praesentes* "Sed quando praesentibus monialibus districtior vita imponi potuit?"

32. *Decretum* C. 32 q. 1 c. 13. The rubric reads: "Virginitas ex consilio suadetur, non ex imperio precipitur."

own wills and so can have imposed on them a rule of life stricter than the one they presently follow.[33]

Joannes uses Clement V's decree *Ne in agro dominico* as the principal support for his conclusion. Issued at the Council of Vienne (1311–12), the decree consisted of very detailed (if far from new) stipulations about the food, dress, and comportment of monks, set down so that "nothing unbecoming or corrupt find its way into that field of the Lord, namely the sacred order of the black monks."[34] The pope prescribed the quality and color of the cloth for monastic habits, stipulated that the sleeves extend to the hands and be neither sewn nor buttoned, forbade the wearing of ornate belts, knives, or spurs, and the use of ornamented saddles and bridles. Footwear, the keeping of hunting-dogs or birds, and the minimum age for administrators were all considered appropriate topics for legislation. Interestingly, *Ne in agro dominico* even used language reminiscent of *Periculoso* in discussing the problem of wandering monks: "Some monks, as we hear, throw off the sweet yoke of regular observance and leave their monasteries, feigning that they cannot securely remain there, or under some other pretext, to wander about the courts of princes."[35] Monks who visit said courts, or engage in "any wandering about" *(quisbuslibet vagationibus et discursu)* were to be severely corrected by their superiors.

Having cited this prestigious authority to support his assertion that the papacy could prescribe the way of life for monks and nuns regardless of the nature of their existing rules, Joannes then makes two significant additions that appear to undercut his previous argument. First, he refers the reader to the hallowed rule of law incorporated into the *Liber Sextus:* "what touches all must be approved by all," leaving the impression that while the individual monk or nun (as opposed to

33. "Vel dic, supradicta vera in clericus secularibus; in religiosus qui velle vel nolle non habent, secus quia illis potest strictior vita indici, etiam ex regula secundum."

34. *Clem* 3.10.1 "Ne in agro dominico sacra videlicet monachorum nigorum religione, indecorum aliquid obrepat aut vitiosum . . ."

35. "Quia vero nonnulli monachorum ipsorum, sicut accepimus, suavi iugo observantiae regularis abiecto, interdum, propriis relictis monasteriis, se in secure morari non posse fingentes, vel alio colore quaesito, per curias principum evagando discurrunt."

the secular clerk) had surrendered his will at profession, the consent of the body, the monastic community as a whole, might be needed to put even papal decrees like *Periculoso* into effect.[36] Second, he adds that although it is clear that the pope may make many laws governing the so-called goods of fortune, that is, monastic food, clothing, comportment, and the like (preserving the essence of the monastic rule of course), he is not so empowered to regulate the goods of nature, grace, or glory, which God alone controls.[37]

As if to compensate for introducing such ambiguity, Joannes concludes this section by calling for uniform observance of the specific legislation embodied in *Periculoso*. He notes that regardless of variations in locale, variation in the law ought not be tolerated since it is said that the pope holds sway over the whole world.[38] Citing Pope Gelasius I, Joannes endorses the full-blown ideal of papal supremacy, including the right of people from the world over to petition for papal justice— a justice from which there is no appeal.

No matter how staunchly Joannes would like to support the doctrine of papal supremacy and the pope's authority to legislate, however, he is required to leave room for individual conscience. As noted with reference to Joannes Monachus, Gratian and the Decretists had

36. *VI* 5.13.29 "Quod omnes tangit debet ab omnibus approbari." I shall discuss the ramifications of citing this Roman law maxim at the conclusion of this chapter.

37. "Additio. Et per haec iura patet Papam circa professos multum posse in cibis, vestibus, modo manendi, et similibus, quae plus cadunt in bonis fortunae, reservata tamen naturali sustentatione et substantialibus regulae, de quibus dicitur supra, eodem [refering to *Ne in agro dominico* cited above; he also cites here the end of *X* 3.35.6 which reads: "Ne aestimet abbas, quod super habenda proprietate possit cum aliquo monacho dispensare; quia abdicatio proprietatis, sicut et custodia castitatis, adeo est annexa regulae monachali, ut contra eam nec summus Pontifex possit licentiam indulgere."] In bonis autem naturae, gratiae, vel gloriae, non est tanta Papae potentia, quod per se patet; illa enim Deus cuius vices gerit, non transtulit in eum."

38. *GO* to *VI* 3.16.1 v.*partibus* "Quia varietas locorum, iuris varietatem regulariter non inducit . . . Et nota quod dicit mundi, totius enim orbis Papa tenet principatum . . ." Pope Gelasius I is alleged next: *Decretum* C. 9 q. 3 c. 17–18, mentioning, as illustrative of universal papal authority, the right of appeal: "Si quidem ad illam de qualibet mundi parte appellandum est; ab illa autem nemo est appellare permissus . . ."

conceded the importance of granting permission to a monk or nun to leave one religious house and enter another more austere order, since the urgings of one's conscience took precedence over the letter of the law. The same attitude is clearly apparent in Joannes Andreae's statement that, although *Periculoso* prescribes perpetual claustration of nuns, it does not prohibit them from leaving their monasteries for the purpose of entering a stricter order.[39] Further refinements of *Periculoso*, largely clarifications, follow. Joannes notes that those nuns who were not already professed at the time *Periculoso* was published were not held to obey it.[40] He strictly interprets the somewhat vague notions expressed by the words: "and that no person, in any way disreputable, or even respectable shall be allowed to enter or leave . . . unless a reasonable and just cause exists."[41] Given that Boniface VIII prohibited even the most respectable outsiders from entering the cloister unlicensed, Joannes concludes that even monks ought not enter convents, nor should they speak with individual nuns save in the presence of the abbess, and then briefly.[42] Joannes defines a "reasonable and just cause" for entrance into the cloister as the need for the services of select specialists such as physicians, barbers, seamstresses, or carpenters.[43]

Joannes approaches his next subject, monastic poverty, with a respect and interest colored by his times. As we have seen, Boniface had determined that nunneries, save for mendicant communities, were to

39. *GO* to *VI* 3.16.1 v.*perpetua* "Non credo quod decretalis ista tollat, quin possent, si vellent ad strictiorem religionem humilitatis et puritatis causa transire . . . Item quin una monialis ad regimen alterius monasterii possit assumi." Citing *X* 3.31.18, Joannes does add that a license from the ordinary must first be procured for such a transfer.

40. *GO* to *VI* 3.16.1 v.*professae* "si ergo professa non erat huius constitutionis, tempore non tenetur." He adduces *VI* 3.14.3 that refers to mendicants who are required to allow a probationary year to elapse before admitting a new member.

41. "nullique aliquatenus inhonestae personae nec etiam honestae (nisi rationalibus et manifesta causa exsistat . . .) ingressus vel accessus pateat ad easdem, . . ."

42. *GO* to *VI* 3.16.1 v.*honestae* "Unde nec monachi ad eas accedere debent, vel cum eis colloqui, nisi in praesentia abbatissae per modica verba . . ."

43. *GO* to *VI* 3.16.1 v.*causa* "Sicut in medicis, barbitonsoribus, sartoribus, carpentariis cum eguerint, et his similibus."

admit new members only when their resources were adequate to sustain them; that is, if the expanded community could continue to function without being reduced to penury. If a nun was admitted to a community that had inadequate resources, her religious profession was void.

Joannes accepts the pope's reasoning but immediately cautions against too liberal an interpretation. Wealth, and thus poverty, he notes, are relative things, and attitudes toward them are conditioned by personal status and regional custom. It is significant, therefore, that Boniface did not use the words "comfortably sustain" but only "able to sustain" when speaking of a community's means. To illustrate, Joannes cites the example of the canons of Bologna, who might not be able to sustain themselves comfortably on 100 florins, yet who could live without being reduced to penury on 25. Penury, he adds, denotes indigence, the lack of even the necessities of life, and *Periculoso* is worded simply to keep all but mendicant communities from begging for the basics of life. Just because a community is not comfortably endowed, however, does not mean it cannot accept new members.[44]

Joannes apparently appreciates the fact that women as well as men might be prepared to forego a comfortable standard of living as the price for joining a specific community that they admired. Nevertheless,

44. *GO* to *VI* 3.16.1 v.*absque penuria* "Nota non dixit commode, nam in quadam questione de facto opponebatur contra quasdam moniales quod earum receptio non tenebat quia facultates non sufficiebant; et formatus fuerat articulus in hec verba: intendit probare, quod ex facultatibus monasterii Sancti Petri non possunt tot commode sustentari. Opposui quod intentio probata non relevabat, quia possunt esse quod non possent commode, tamen possent absque penuria; iam enim dico quod canonicus Bononiensis de centum florenis non posset commode sustentari, et tamen de 25 sustentarentur absque penuria. Idem dico de meipso, nam in illa commoditate inspicitur consuetudo regionis, et qualitas personae, unde licet non possum commode sustentari, tamen possum sine penuria. Penuria enim secundum derivatores habent in se aegestatem, indigentiam, et defectum necessariorum. Hoc ergo voluit constitutio, quod constitutae in monasterio non mendicantium non haberent necesse mendicare propter necessarium defectu. Si autem considerato antiquo statu monasterii, vel aliis monasteriis civitatis, non possunt commode sustentari, tamen possunt absque penuria, tenebit receptio: hoc enim ius novum, quod receptionem vitiat, extendendum non est, et sic obtinuit."

"in conjunction with Joannes Monachus and the Archdeacon," he stresses that the consequences for men admitted to communities too poor to maintain their numbers adequately would be completely different than for women. A monk's religious vows would not be void under such circumstances since monks, unlike nuns, could readily venture outside the cloister to secure the necessities that they required to survive.[45]

A curious and, one might contend, genuinely academic question is added by Joannes to this discussion of communal poverty: What is to be done if virgins, calling themselves (reformed) whores, enter a monastery founded exclusively to receive penitent prostitutes? Their reception, according to one Johannes de Deo, is null and void, and when their fraud is discovered they should be expelled.[46] While recent research shows that considerable effort was made to reform prostitutes in the thirteenth and fourteenth centuries within convents founded for repentant women, the specific situation proposed by this hypothesis was probably uncommon.[47] Nevertheless, it is often cited by subsequent canonists, suggesting that women might have used some such ploy to flout *Periculoso*'s limitations on the number of nuns permitted in more traditional religious communities.

The timely topic of communal poverty seems to have piqued Joannes Andreae's interest, and his detailed discussion of enforcement of *Periculoso* reflects similar engagement. In his decree, Boniface VIII applied the principles of papal supremacy that would be sharpened in his conflict with the king of France. The pope asserted his right to

45. *GO* to *VI* 3.16.1 v.*irritum* "Hoc speciale dictum videtur in talibus monasteriis foeminarum, secus puto in monasteriis virorum. Idem Joan. Monac. et Archd. licet enim et in illis ultra quam sustentari possunt, recipi non debeant: si tamen fuerint recepti, tendebit: quia et hominum possunt."

46. *GO* to *VI* 3.16.1 *additio* post v.*irritum* "quod si virgines dicentes se meretrices, ingrediuntur monasterium institutum ad recipiendas solas meretrices poenitentes et non alias, non tenet receptio, nec possunt ibi salvari fraude durante, qua revelata inde debent expelli." Johannes de Deo is probably the Portugese canonist who studied at Bologna in the mid 13th century, see: *DDC* vol. 6 p. 99.

47. See Brundage, *Law, Sex, and Christian Society,* pp. 463–69, for an overview of the subject as treated by canonists from 1234 to 1348; also, Leah Otis, "Prostitution," vol. 10, *DMA,* pp. 154–55.

require civil authorities to help enforce cloister regulations and he stressed the obligation of secular lords to allow nuns to conduct their monastic business, even as it pertained to oaths of fealty or homage, by proxy. Sensitive to the practical implications of these rulings, Joannes Andreae sought to clarify the jurisdictional divisions whenever possible.

He asks first under what circumstances an abbess might leave her monastery to do homage on behalf of her community to a temporal lord, underscoring the fact that such personal appearances should be necessary *only* in the case of temporal lords since all ecclesiastical overlords would be expected to receive proctors in these cases.[48] Raising the old issue of simony only to lay it quickly to rest, Joannes distinguishes between the spiritual and temporal components of a monastic holding. Citing the eleventh rule of law from the *Decretals of Gregory IX:* "homage must not be performed for spiritualities," he explains that a nun must not do homage in return for receiving properties that carried with them an obligation to provide spiritual services, since that would involve the sin of simony.[49] Obviously wishing to encourage the use of proctors whenever possible, Joannes makes his point in three separate entries. Glossing the word *praestet* he adduces an oath to defend papal holdings, taken by no less a figure than the Ottonian Henry I, as support for the legitimacy of promises by proxy.[50]

Personal appearances in secular courts pose threats to the law of enclosure, and Joannes cites another of Boniface VIII's constitutions, adduced by Joannes Monachus and also found in the *Liber Sextus,* for support.[51] In it the pope sets forth in unambiguous language his ruling

48. *GO* to *VI* 3.16.1 v.*Domino temporali* "In ecclesiastico enim secus, quia ille necessitate, illas per procuratorem ad hoc faciendum admittere debet . . ."
49. *GO* to *VI* 3.16.1 v.*homagium.* He cites Gregory IX *X* 5.41.11 "Pro spiritualibus homagium non praestatur," then, for the *solutio* cites *X* 5.3.17 "pro habendis spiritualibus homagium facere simoniacum est.
50. *GO* to *VI* 3.16.1 v.*praestet* "Et sic iuratur per procuratorem, ut de hoc . . ." [*Decretum* D. 6 c. 33 the rubric of which reads "Iuramenteum Ottonis, [Henry I] quod fecit domino Papae Johanni." This text performs "double duty" since it testifies to papal might as well—Henry I promised to defend the lands of St. Peter and to undertake no action regarding Rome or papal interests without the pope's counsel.
51. *GO* to *VI* 3.16.1 v.*tractari* "Sed nonne hoc est ius commune omnium

that when not expressly required by law, women were not to be compelled to go to courts of law against their wills, and that religious women, even if they *are* willing, should not be required to make personal appearances before a judge. Depositions taken by a judge's official might satisfy the court's needs in some cases; in others a judge might have to make a special trip to hear the pleading of a female principal. Whatever the inconvenience, however, it was to be negotiated since laxity in a judge might incur the sentence of excommunication. Joannes notes the relative leniency of *Periculoso* on this issue of sanctions—in that decree Boniface VIII had *not* threatened uncompliant secular lords with excommunication if they persisted in demanding that an abbess appear personally in their courts. He attempts to account for that leniency by saying that perhaps the professional status of a judge placed greater responsibility upon him, thus making delinquency a matter of more severe punishment.[52]

Although Joannes argues that it is the *ius commune* that women in general not be held to appear personally at court, he is forced to admit (as Boniface VIII himself had admitted) that there are occasions when a journey by the head of a female monastic community to render homage or fealty could not be avoided. When commenting on those occasions, Joannes advises strict regulation. The abbess, he states, must always travel in the company of two or more aged monks and her chaplain.[53] Her entourage is to be above suspicion and their return to the monastery immediate, allowing no time for indiscretion.[54]

---

mulierum, quod personaliter non trahantur ad iudicium, super eodem libro . . ." He cites *VI* 2.1.2 the rubric of which reads: "Mulieres personaliter ad iudicium quacumque causa, in iure non expressus, invitae trahendae non sunt; sed si necessarium sit ipsarum testimonium in causa, iudex expensis producentis interdum ibit, interdum mittet; et iudex fraudulenter vadens excommunicatus est. Mulieres religiosae, etiam volentes, extra monasterium suum ex aliqua causa personaliter ad iudicium trahi non possunt. Quod contra praedicta fit, est irritum."

52. *GO* to *VI* 3.16.1 v.*fraudem* "Sic supra eodem libro [*VI* 2.1.2] Sed ibi poena excommunicationis imponitur, hic non forte ratio fuit iudicialis auctoritas, propter quam ibi magis delinquitur."

53. *GO* to *VI* 3.16.1 v.*societate* "Habebit secum duas, vel plures ex antiquis monachabus et capellanos suos, et incedat honeste."

54. *GO* to *VI* 3.16.1 v.*E vestigio* "Id est statim vel continuo."

The *Glossa Ordinaria*'s discussion of *Periculoso* concludes with firm statements on the right of the papacy to compel secular rulers to support his position. Boniface noted the "peril of souls" that might arise if religious women wandered abroad, even on missions connected with their feudal obligations. According to Joannes it is on this basis, as guardian of spiritual persons and matters, that the pope is empowered to make rulers comply with his decree.[55] So too, the secular arm might be invoked to assist the papacy in all its good works, not to prejudice lay authority, but in order to carry out what is pleasing to God.[56]

The earliest set of commentary on *Periculoso,* culminating in that cogent distillation, the *Glossa Ordinaria,* was not monolithic. There were ambiguities and discrepancies within and among the glosses. The short commentaries of Joannes Monachus and Guido de Baysio gave way to the detailed work of Joannes Andreae; Joannes Monachus' single-minded attention to the juridical aspects of enforcement hardly mattered to Guido de Baysio; Joannes Andreae could not be content with Joannes Monachus's deft solution to the problem of nuns being asked to live under a rule of life stricter than the one under which they had entered.

Nevertheless, the combined work of these early glossators laid the foundation for all subsequent commentary. It not only set standards and provided a pattern for later commentators, but also focused attention on particular questions that became recognized as central to any discussion of *Periculoso.* Subsequent canonists could, and would, shift their angle of vision, yet they would all begin their works with a recognition that their predecessors had already grappled with some of the most important legal/moral issues posed by *Periculoso.* Those issues included: the limits of papal prerogative, corporate poverty, the claims that both the law and the spirit had upon the individual Christian, and the related issue of the spiritual equality of monks and nuns.

55. *GO* to *VI* 3.16.1 v.*Inducat* "Merito igitur potuit papa super hoc legem dare ad idem, supra eodem libro . . ." He cites *VI* 2.2.3 and *VI* 2.11.1, both dealing with ecclesiastical jurisdiction when matters spiritual are at stake.

56. *GO* to *VI* 3.16.1 v.*secularis* "et exhibebitur non ad preiudicandum, sed ad que Deo sunt placita exequendum." In support Joannes cites *X* 1.31.1 the rubric of which reads: "Episcopi in suis dioecesibus possunt crimina inquirere et punire, et, quum opus fuerit, invocare brachium saeculare."

Periculoso's innovative approach to claustration—via papal mandate—made it a natural focus for discussion of papal prerogative.[57] Unanimously accepting the pope's authority to legislate for all nuns throughout Christendom, the early glossators expressed their support for a doctrine of papal supremacy. Joannes Monachus unabashedly claimed for *Periculoso*'s papal sanctions the force of excommunication, and Joannes Andreae reveled in adducing citations in support of the pope's right to enlist the aid of secular rulers as well as that of the clergy. The importance that Joannes Andreae attached to the un-coerced entrance into religion, while admitting that the rules of religious life could be changed at the behest of a pope, suggests the level of respect he had for papal prerogative. Furthermore, this "profession of faith" in papal power was not undermined by the citation of the Roman law maxim: "what touches all must be approved by all." *Periculoso* had clearly not been approved by all the communities of nuns it strove to regulate, but medieval lawyers, who had adapted this rule of law (originally designed to govern the affairs of a minor with two or more guardians) to apply to corporate bodies, and indeed to the Latin church at large, would not have found that fact in any way troublesome.[58] Using the mechanism of mandated powers of representation—representation via proctor, or, in English law, proxy—the lawyers taught that some small group, such as the college of cardinals or cathedral canons, could give the necessary consent on their behalf. Moreover, "consent" in this context implied no challenge to the superior right of the pope to make final decisions.[59]

Periculoso's ruling about limiting the number of nuns within cloistered communities gave at least one of the canonists, Joannes Andreae, an opportunity not only to discuss the rationale for such a limitation but to comment on an issue much in the air: corporate poverty. A layman, possibly influenced by the zeal of the friars, his gloss betrayed a

57. On the later medieval canonists and their ideas about the principles governing the exercise of papal power see especially: Kenneth Pennington, *The Prince and the Law, 1200–1600.*

58. On the medieval adaptation of *quod omnes tangit* see Gaines Post, *Studies in Medieval Legal Thought,* chap. 4.

59. Post, *Studies,* pp. 4 and 164ff., illustrates the way in which papal prerogative remained intact, despite the requirements of *quod omnes tangit.*

bias in favor of monastic life limited to its essentials. *Periculoso* also provided the early glossators with a forum for discussion of the tension between so-called private and public law; it allowed them to point up the distinctions between the need for legal restriction and discipline coupled with the obligation to recognize the spiritual liberty granted by the message of Christ.

This weighty issue surfaced in two separate places in the commentarial literature. First, it was bound up with the question of whether a nun transfering to a stricter order would be considered in violation of Boniface VIII's cloister rulings. It is impossible to know whether Joannes Andreae grafted this question onto a discussion of *Periculoso* because he felt that the occurrence was widespread enough to be of particular concern to ordinaries, because he was following Joannes Monachus's lead, or because he felt that the issue of freedom of conscience that traditionally surrounded its discussion was worth keeping in view. Whatever the rationale, from the time of the publication of the *Glossa Ordinaria* transfer to a stricter order would be seen by the canonists as one of the justifiable exceptions to *Periculoso*.

Second, and less obviously, distinctions between the spirit and the letter of the law arose when the commentators distinguished between monks and nuns. On the one hand, ecclesiastical tradition accepted the essential similarity of the spiritual needs of monks and nuns; on the other hand, *Periculoso* had decreed a change in policy for nuns alone. The earliest canonists grappled with this paradox in different ways. Joannes Monachus stressed that men and women were distinctly different at law. Women were under certain categorical disadvantages, and proof texts from Roman as well as canon law put this conclusion beyond debate. Women in general, not trusted to act in their own best interests, were to be kept out of the public gaze, whether that scrutiny involved appearance in a court of law or mendicancy. Strict cloister regulations, such as prescribed by Boniface VIII, were thus feasible and indeed advisable for nuns, who had the added obligation of protecting their chastity. For Guido de Baysio, approaching *Periculoso* from a moral and not a purely legal standpoint, the issue was not so straightforward. Guido placed heavy emphasis on the words, *modestia* and *verecundia,* that Boniface had used of the virtues essential to nuns. He analyzed the virtue of purity and argued that it was essential to women. Yet he could not link *Periculoso*'s cloister regulations directly to the need to preserve female chastity, because he could not ignore traditional injunctions recommending some form of enclosure for the spiritual welfare of monks as well as nuns. The result was a curious incongruity. Joannes Andreae clearly approved of his teacher's placement of emphasis. He too paid special attention to the notion of "nunnish modesty." He expanded upon the Archdeacon's distinctions and cited further proof texts for his definitions: St. Augustine as well as the Old Testament on the veil as a symbol of female modesty; corruption occasioned not only by sexual intercourse but also by lewd kisses and caresses; monastic vows as analogous to marriage vows and Christ the spouse as akin to the earthly husband. By omitting any mention of analogous recommendations to monks, however, Joannes Andreae did imply that the strict enclosure rules of *Periculoso* were there to safeguard female chastity. He then went on to elaborate those regulations.

Whereas Boniface VIII had been somewhat vague in describing the type of person who might enter a monastery of nuns and the reasons for that entrance, Joannes was specific—not even monks might enter unlicensed; no conversation could occur save in the presence of the abbess. "Reasonable and just cause" for entry was delimited as the need for services of specialists such as physicans, barbers, seamstresses, or carpenters. He similarly clarified or added to *Pericloso*'s rules regarding egress. Like Joannes Monachus, he explained that *Periculoso* had placed limits on the number of nuns permitted in any given house because nuns, as opposed to monks, could not beg for, or in other ways publicly procure, their necessities of life. He prescribed the exact nature of the entourage of an abbess forced to leave her monastery to satisfy feudal obligations: two or more aged monks and her chaplain, and he put much emphasis on the use of proctors to obviate this necessity.

With the work of Joannes Andreae then, the canonical elaboration of the differences, at law, between male and female monastics had begun in earnest. Although removal from the cares and temptations of the world was still, in theory, essential to the spiritual life of monks, that ideal would recede further and further into the background for the commentators. Their legal status as men—which included responsibilities such as maintaining financial solvency, as well as liberties, such as being free to embrace the priesthood—made it impossible for cloister laws to be so perfectly applied to monks. Joannes Andreae's citation of Clement V's decree, *Ne in agro dominico,* with its talk of monks riding, hunting, and frequenting the courts of princes, actually served to point up this fact. Moreover, nuns had their chastity to preserve. Strict enclosure regulations with elaborate and specific guidelines for entrance to and exit from the monastery, and not just the general advice of St. Benedict to remain aloof from worldly concerns, would be the only true safeguard for that virtue of unique importance to women. Guido de Baysio had not been ready to make such a clear-cut distinction between monks and nuns—in the *Glossa Ordinaria,* Joannes Andreae was.

F I V E

Commentary from the *Glossa Ordinaria*

through the Fourteenth Century

The *Glossa Ordinaria* to the *Liber Sextus* became an indispensable companion to Boniface VIII's work. Although it drew on the comments of Joannes Monachus and Guido de Baysio, as we have seen, the lengthy gloss soon overshadowed their more modest contributions. It served as a virtual template for subsequent canonists, who, although not slavish imitators, most often confined their own comments to words cited by the ordinary gloss. Not content with his achievement, however, Joannes Andreae went on to write another lengthy (500,000 words) commentary on the *Liber Sextus*. Between 1336 and 1342 Joannes composed the *Novella in Sextum*.[1] Judging from the number of times it is cited, this work too became very popular among contempories, and although it often alludes to the *Glossa Ordinaria* (as might be expected), it contains sufficient original material to be of interest here.

In the *Novella*, as in the ordinary gloss, Joannes's discussion of *Peri-*

---

1. See chap. 4 for biographical details on Joannes Andreae; I have used the 1499 edition of the *Novella in Sextum* (Venetiis: P. Pincius), reprinted in 1963 (Graz: Akademische Druck- u. Verlagsanstalt), hereafter cited as *Novella* in *VI*.

culoso begins with an obeisance to his teacher Guido de Baysio. In addition to repeating his master's definition of *periculoso* he reiterates Guido's definition of *verecundia* (when glossing the words *extra sua [monasteria]*) as well. In the *Glossa Ordinaria*, Joannes had elaborated upon and clarified *Periculoso*'s regulations based on the tacit assumption that nuns required such strict cloister regulations to enable them to preserve their most important virtue—chastity. Having established this distinction between monks and nuns, he now cites the Archdeacon's statement—apparently confident that it will be seen as merely a counsel to perfection—that leaving the confines of the cloister is prohibited by ancient authority even to monks.[2] Joannes next adduces a well-known citation from the *Decretum* banning double monasteries, to emphasize that *Periculoso* validly restricts the entrance of suspect persons into the cloister.[3] If even monks are forbidden to fraternize with nuns, how much less seculars are to be trusted! He also clarifies what *Periculoso* means when it states that violating enclosure, either by admitting outsiders or by leaving the monastery, injures "those who by free choice vowed their chastity *[integritatem]*." *Integritatem*, he says, refers both to virginity and to continence; thus St. Paul counsels not only virgins but also widows to take care to remain faithful to their religious profession.[4]

A new and interesting discussion, one that subsequent canonists will be drawn into time and again, follows next. Joannes says that it appears *Periculoso* has not been received in parts of France, and for whatever reasons, its provisions are not kept in Venice. In view of this laxness, he continues, the Archdeacon thinks that abbesses should not be allowed to make visits to the monasteries under their jurisdiction, but rather that visitations to enforce cloister regulations should be

2. *Novella* in *VI* 3.16.1 v.*periculoso* "Et Archdiaconus exponit *periculoso*, id est pernicioso, detestabili, id est execrabili. *Verecundia* est pudor vel timor propter que cessatur ab illicitis et hic ingenuos prodit natales . . .'"; v. *extra sua*, hec prohibetur etiam maribus.

3. *Novella* in *VI* 3.16.1 v.*admittunt*; he adduces *Decretum* C. 18 q. 2 c.21 the rubric of which reads: "Cum sanctimonialibus monachis habitare non licet."

4. *Novella* in *VI* 3.16.1 v.*integritatem* "id est virginitatem vel continentiam." Joannes cites *Decretum* C 27 q 1 c 1–2 refering to vowed widows as well as virgins.

made by others assigned the role.[5] In support, he cites the decree *Attendentes* of Clement V, which provides for such visits to female houses and which specifically states that those who in any way hinder the visitors in their task, unless they repent on being admonished, should incur excommunication.[6]

Joannes goes on to buttress the Archdeacon's reasoning. He points out that it is an accepted legal maxim that "what is written in general terms be understood in general terms." One marries, for example, accepting the fact that under normal circumstances, marriage is indissoluble and that only special circumstance would allow for spouses to separate—Joannes cites the *Decretals of Gregory IX* on the contraction of leprosy by one spouse to illustrate his argument about exceptional circumstances.[7] Although *Periculoso* does not speak specifically about abbesses in the passage under discussion, when it refers to nuns it includes abbesses as well, just as the term "monk" encompasses abbots. Consequently, if abbesses, as nuns, are to be under strict cloister regulations, they certainly cannot be responsible for conducting visitations to insure that those rules are respected by others. Adding further support to his argument, Joannes notes that in paragraph two of his decree, Boniface actually *does* mention abbesses and requires them to travel in respectable and decent company if they must leave the monastery for the purpose of doing homage or swearing fealty.[8]

On a related issue, the question of special licenses for entrance to or exit from the cloister, Joannes inserts a telling etymology. Reasserting the peculiar importance of chastity for women religious, he says

5. *Novella* in *VI* 3.16.1 v.*partibus:* "fertur quod hec constitutio recepta non fuit in partibus gallicanis; vidi etiam ipsam non servari Venetiis quacumque ratione vel causa. Per hoc putat Archdiaconus quod etiam pro visitandis monasteriis sibi subiectis abbatissa egredi non possit; faciat igitur visitationem per alium, et vide quod notat in Clementinas . . ."

6. *Clem* 3.10.2.

7. "quia generaliter scriptum generaliter accipiendum, supra *X* 4.8.2"; Joannes also cites other instances where an exception is made to a general rule: a privilege of exemption from tithes (*X* 3.30.12), and a concession to widows allowing remarriage *Decretum* (C 31 q 1 c 10).

8. "Et si dicatur quod ista littera non loquitur de abbatissa, respondet quod appellatio monachi includit abbates ubi de animarum salute agitur . . ."; *Novella* in *VI* 3.16.1 v.*verum*" *VI* 3.16.1 & 2 exprimit de abbatissa, et manifesta."

that *Periculoso* sometimes uses the word *sanctimoniales* to refer to nuns, and that that word underscores their purported holiness *(sanctitas)*—a holiness that is *synonymous* with chastity *(castitas)*. [9]

A reasonably long section follows, based on *Periculoso*'s exhortations to secular rulers. Boniface had asked temporal lords to allow nuns to carry out any administrative business or to litigate in their tribunals through the agency of proctors or attorneys. Joannes uses this passage as an occasion to address the ever-delicate issue of ecclesiastical and secular jurisdiction. He musters numerous allegations to corroborate the general principle that clerks should be tried in church courts and that in all matters spiritual, canonical jurisdiction be respected. [10]

Warning that any court activity contains within it the potential for evil-doing, he cites Clement V's decree admonishing monks to avoid the courts of princes—if they go there in spite of his restrictions, and do so in order to cause harm to their superiors or to their monasteries, Clement declares them automatically excommunicated. [11] Joannes seems to have seen special merit in Clement V's method of exacting obedience, since when glossing the word *acrimoniam*—the term which Boniface VIII used to refer to his sanctions against those who failed to accept *Periculoso*—Joannes unhesitatingly defines it as excommunication. [12]

After a series of curt allusions (with almost no alteration in content)

9. *Novella* in *VI* 3.16.1 v. *speciali* "id est ad hoc specialiter perita et obtenta, Archdiaconus."; v.*sanctimonio* "alias *sanctimonia,* id est sanctitate vel castitate et ab hac sanctimoniales dicuntur."

10. *Novella* in *VI* 3.16.1 v. *occasionem* he cites *X* 1.33.6, the rubric of which reads: "Imperium non praeest sacerdotio, sed subest, et ei obedire tenetur. Vel sic: Episcopus non debet subesse principibus, sed praeesse."; v. *seu curiis* he cites *Decretum* C. 11 q. 1 c. 10, the rubric of which reads: "Si quis clericus accusans clericum in curia introierit anathema sit." as well as *VI* 5.11.8, the rubric of which reads: "Iudex ecclesiasticus compellet iudicem laicum, repellere excommunicatos ab actibus iudiciariis sibi prohibitis."

11. *Novella* in *VI* 3.16.1 v.*curias principum* "Ad reprehensionem curiarum dixit: 'Curia curarum genetrix, nutrixque malorum.'" Joannes cites *Clem* 3.10.1.

12. *Novella* in *VI* 3.16.1 v.*acrimoniam* "id est excommunicationem"; note that Joannes follows Joannes Monachus in this definition "vel secundum Joannem Monachum componitur ab *acer* et *moneo* quasi acris monitio, et designat austeritatem in vultu."

to topics he had already discussed in the *Glossa Ordinaria,* Joannes choose to expand on one of them. He begins by reviewing the hypothetical case proposed by Johannes de Deo, about the reception of virgins posing as penitent prostitutes, into an order founded exclusively for the latter.[13] In the *Glossa Ordinaria* Joannes had concluded that if the virgins were discovered, they were to be expelled from the community. He now elaborates his position. Citing the words of St. Augustine, Joannes contends that even a desire to be humble does not excuse deceit—falsely claiming that you have committed some grave sin, for instance, out of a misplaced sense of humility, merits you nothing.[14] Veracity is essential to virtuous acts, witness the disaster that befell Jeroboam's wife when, by disguising herself, she tried to deceive the prophet Ahijah.[15] In fact, even otherwise sinful deeds, such as eating meat during Lent, may be allowed if necessity intervenes and one is right-minded, that is, imbued with the upright man's fear of committing sin.[16]

Joannes next poses a question of his own: What if a community of virgins that already contains the maximum number of nuns that can be supported without lapsing into penury, decides, neverthless, to accept some (penitent) prostitutes? Acccording to Joannes, this would be violating *Periculoso,* trying to circumvent its provisions by accepting a type of woman (no matter how wealthy) whom the founders of the house had never intended to admit. The purpose for which a religious house was founded must always be respected, since things must be used for their intended ends.

13. *Novella* in *VI* 3.16.1 v.*irritum* ". . . pro Joanne de Deo, liber iii questio x, tenuit quod si virgines dicentes se meretrices ingrediuntur monasterium institutum ad recipiendas solum meretrices penitentes et non alias, non teneat receptio, nec possunt ibi salvari fraude durante; que revelata inde debent expelli . . ."

14. The sermon of St. Augustine is cited from the *Decretum* C. 22 q. 2 c. 9; it concludes with the words: "Nam quomodo est humilitas, ubi regnat falsitas?"

15. 1 Kings 14; Joannes also cites *Decretum* C. 33 q. 1 c. 2 where the consequences of lying about one's inability to consummate a marriage are discussed.

16. *X* 3.46.2: ". . . ne ipsis aliquatenus imputetur quia bonarum mentium est, ibi timere culpam, ubi culpa minime reperitur . . ."

To support this position, Joannes again alleges Clement V. Railing against those who, while in charge of hospices, leper-houses, or hospitals, have allowed them to fall into disrepair, the pope especially condemns the diverting of revenues intended for these charitable institutions since "that which has been given by the faithful for a certain purpose should, except by authority of the apostolic see, be applied to that purpose and no other."[17] Finally, Joannes admits that an institution might occasionally have two mandates, a dual purpose, just as a prison might serve a custodial as well as a penal function.[18] It is implied that, were a convent to have such dual function, admission of the penitential prostitutes would be permitted.

The *Novella*'s treatment of *Periculoso* ends with a few traditional cautions about the kind of companions (old and above suspicion) that an abbess should have if she needs to step outside of her cloister.[19] *Periculoso* required the speedy return of the abbess, no matter how well companioned, and Joannes leaves no room for a liberal interpretation. *Ex vestigio* were the words used in *Periculoso;* they were the same words used in a law from the *Digest* concerning the length of time a husband had to return a dowry to his estranged wife. In both cases, he contends, they meant *immediately.*[20]

In his *Novella,* Joannes Andreae continued to develop themes that had emerged in the *Glossa Ordinaria.* He specifically developed the theme of female purity. Purity became *the* virtue for nuns; it was the "holiness" in the term "holy nuns." Nor was it solely virginity that

17. "Si per virgines occupentur loca monasterii ad numerum quo plures non possunt absque penuria sustentari, auferetur ingrediendi facultas meretricibus penitere volentibus cum ipsarum receptio non teneret per hunc et sic remanebunt in peccato et fiet contra mentem instituentis locum optime facit." Joannes cites *Clem* 3.11.2 v. *cum tamen:* ". . . cum tamen ea, quae ad certum usum largitione sunt destinata fidelium, ad illum debeant non ad alium, salva quidem sedis apostolicae auctoritate, converti."

18. *VI* 5.9.3 the rubric of which reads: "Quamvis inventio carceris fuerit ad custodiam, tamen potest quis punire poena carceris perpetuo et ad tempus."

19. *Novella* in *VI* 3.16.1 v.*societate* "antiquis, videlicet enim etas ad suspitionem tollendam."

20. *Novella* in *VI* 3.16.1 v.*e vestigio* Joannes cites *Digest* 3.5.34. A husband, according to this law, was guilty of wrongdoing if he did not immediately sell his property in order to obtain the amount equivalent to his wife's dowry.

needed protection. *Integritas,* the chastity of the widow and even the penitent prostitute, was to be guarded by new, strict, cloister regulations—regulations that Joannes worked out in detail. Even though he was a layman, Joannes's attitude toward the preservation of the chastity of nuns was as rigorous as that of any celibate cleric. He expanded upon the somewhat general stipulations of *Periculoso* aimed at guarding that chastity, and did not seem to feel that the new strict rules that were being imposed upon women religious should be in any way mitigated. Another layman and contemporary, Petrus de Ancarano, was not so sure.

Born near Orvieto in about 1330, Petrus studied at Bologna with some of the other luminaries of his generation such as Franciscus Zabarella and Antonio de Butrio, and took his doctorate in both laws in 1370.[21] Unlike so many of his predecessors, Petrus did not initially immerse himself fully in academia but held civic offices, among them judge and vicar of the podestà of Bologna, and, from 1384 to 1387, consultant to the Republic of Venice. Subsequently, he did settle into teaching, first at Siena and then, until his death in 1416, at Bologna.

Petrus de Ancarano's work was much admired by contemporaries. It consisted of a vast commentary on the *Decretales* (including the *Liber Sextus*), numerous *consilia* or judicial opinions, and glosses on the *Clementines.*[22] Petrus's commentary on *Periculoso* can still be found in the seventh and final volume of a sixteenth-century edition of his magisterial work on the decretals entitled *Super sexto decretalium acutissima commentaria.* It is organized as a series of eleven headings, each of which corresponds to some notable point in the legislation. Although occupying three folio pages of text, Petrus's gloss is less important as an original work than as an illustration of the hold that the *Glossa Ordinaria* and the *Novella* exerted over generations of continental can-

21. For biographical details see: *DDC* vol. 6 pp. 1464–1470; Smith p. 86; Schulte *QL* vol. 2 pp. 278–82.

22. Two important printed editions of his *Commentaria in Decretales* exist, both of which include his gloss on the *Liber Sextus,* one published at Lyon, 1535–43, another, in seven volumes, published between 1580 and 1583. I will use this edition: *Super Sexto decretalium acutissima commentaria* (Bononiae, apud Societatem typographiae bononiensis, vol. 7 1583); hereafter cited as *Super Sexto decretalium.*

onists. Even when his conclusions diverge, Petrus's debt is betrayed in the overall pattern of comment and the limited range of his discourse.

Petrus begins by noting that nuns are unable to go about outside of their monasteries to visit the homes of seculars, this being prohibited even to men.[23] Although he does cite the "fish out of water" maxim in the tradition of Guido de Baysio, use of the words "even to men," following the usage of the *Novella,* significantly alters the meaning. Instead of suggesting an equality of regulation, the maxim now merely reinforces the notion that nuns, particularly in need of protection, should be particularly bound by rules that even monks are encouraged to follow. Next, after reproducing Joannes Andreae's statement that *Periculoso* is not received in parts of France and not obeyed in Venice, Petrus adds an observation of his own that we can only assume stems from his experiences while in service as Venetian consultant. This state of affairs in Venice, he says, seems to derive from a conflict between the patriarch of Grado and the pope over the enclosure of a group of nuns of the community of *Celestria* who did not wish to be cloistered.[24]

Although citing Clement V's *Ne in agro dominici* to substantiate a pope's ability to legislate for monasteries, Petrus seems to be unwilling to let the issue of individual freedom be submerged in light of stricter enforcement of cloister rules. He cannot resolve the issue as effortlessly as Joannes Monachus who, it will be remembered, contended that *Periculoso* really added nothing new to monastic rules but only addressed the manner in which those rules were to be observed—thus nullifying any objections to living under a monastic rule that in point of fact had become significantly harsher than when one entered the order. Nor does Petrus subscribe to Joannes Andreae's ruthless state-

23. *Super Sexto decretalium* to 3.16.1 par.1 p.354 "Nota, moniales non posse discurrere extra sua monasteria per habitacula secularium hoc etiam prohibetur maribus, *Decretum* C. 16 q. 1 c. 8, 11. Nam secundum regulam beati benedicti monachus inter clausuram morari precipitur et sicut piscis sine aqua caret vita, monachus sine monasterio."

24. *Super Sexto decretalium* to 3.16.1 par.2 p.354 "Dicti Jo. An[dreae] quod ista constitutio non fuit recepta in partibus Gallicanis et vidit etiam ipsam non servare Venetiis. Ubi de hoc vidi questionem inter patriarchem Grandensis datum a Papa visitatorem monasteriorum monialium et moniales de Celestria que nolebat recludi . . ." I have been unable to find out more about the community of Celestria—it is not cited in *Italia Pontificium.*

ment that since monks and nuns are under obedience, they have completely relinquished their own wills.[25]

All religious, Petrus reasons, are initially given a probationary year in order to determine whether the rule of life that they have chosen is too difficult for them; if they find it so, they are permitted to leave. It does not appear, therefore, that religious should be bound to a stricter rule unwillingly; at the very least they should be conceded another probationary year in such circumstances.[26]

Petrus is less of a maverick when treating the issue of exit from the cloister. Following the *Novella* he agrees that even abbesses may not leave their monasteries save for expressed purposes, and that conducting visitations is *not* one of those purposes, since the abbess herself is bound by the rules such visits seek to enforce.[27] Similarly, Petrus subscribes to Joannes Andreae's reasoning about prohibiting suspicious persons from entering a cloistered community: cause for entrance must be clear and reasonable *(manifesta et rationabilis)*, licensed by the ordinary, and confirmed by the bishop.[28] He cites the *Glossa Ordinaria* when repeating the arguments in favor of a strict interpretation of the words *absque penuria*, also echoing Joannes Andreae's opinion that monks need not be bound by the same restrictions.[29]

25. See again, Joannes Monachus, *Glossa aurea* to *VI* 3.16.1 v.*clausura* and Joannes Andreae, *GO* to *VI* 3.16.1 v.*praesentes.*

26. "Sed in contrarium facit, quod ad initio datur annus probationis, ut experiatur asperitates ordinis, infra quem si sibi non placet, possunt exire . . . non ergo videtur, quod contra voluntatum suam ad asperiorem vitam debeat astringi: vel saltem quod concedatur sibi alius annus."

27. *Super Sexto decretalium* to *VI* 3.16.1 par. 3 p.354 "Tangit circa hoc in *Novella* utrum pro visitandis monasteriis sibi subiectis abbatissa possit egredi. Iste tex. facit quod non, quia generaliter loquitur, ergo generaliter debet intelligi . . ."

28. *Super Sexto decretalium* to *VI* 3.16.1 par.4 p.354 ". . . etiam honeste persone prohibentur ingredi clausuram monasterii, nisi subsit manifesta et rationabilis causa et accedat licentia specialis illius ad quem pertinet, puta illius qui preest illi monasterio (*Decretum* C.18 q.2 c.24) qui debet esse ab episcopo comprobatus (*Decretum* C. 18 q. 2 c. 11 . . ."

29. Ibid. par.5 p.354 "..istud verbum *absque penuria* ponderat quod minus importat quam si dixisset *commode sustentari* quod exemplificia ut in glo. super qua dicit . . . In monasterio autem virorum receptio ultra quam possint sine penuria sustentari non vitiat receptionem quam tenet Jo. Mo[nachus] et Arc[hidiaconus]."

When reaffirming the fact that *Periculoso* does allow abbesses to leave their cloisters to perform homage or fealty, Petrus adduces a passage from Gratian declaring that it is fitting that the debtor go to the house of his creditor, rather than have the creditor come to him.[30] He is quick to add, however, that any special privilege lasts only as long as the cause that gave rise to it, and that women in general should not be compelled to come before judges.[31] After repeating Johannes de Deo's hypothetical question concerning virgins posing as penitent prostitutes, Petrus concludes with a question of his own. Following a certain Lapus (Lapus Tactus, associate of Joannes Andreae who wrote in the 1320s), he asks if an exempt monastery might be bound by an episcopal constitution stating that none might enter its confines without the bishop's permission. Lapus doubts that such a decree, especially if it carries with it the threat of excommunication, would be valid.[32] By implication, Petrus agrees. One can only speculate that Petrus includes this *casus* in order to draw a clearer distinction between the powers (even over exempt nunneries) that *Periculoso* conferred on bishops and those which it did not. In this *casus* he underscores the final words of Boniface VIII's decree: "Ordinaries should be aware, however, that they do not acquire in virtue of this [letter] any jurisdiction or power in any other matter over monasteries that are otherwise exempt."

Guido de Baysio gave us our first example of a canonist attempting to come to grips with the spiritual paradox of *Periculoso;* Petrus de Ancarano is an early example of a type that we shall see again, especially

30. Ibid. par.6 p.354. Petrus cites *Decretum* D. 66 c. 1.

31. Ibid. par.7 and 8 p.355.

32. Ibid. par.11 p. 355 "Secundo, quaero post Lap[um] Si monasterium est exemptum et episcopus facit consitutionem ut ad ipsum monasterium nullus accedat sine ipsius licentia sub pena excommunicationis quam ipso facto incurrat: an contrafaciens erit excommunicatus? Videtur quod non. Sicut enim monasterium eximitur ad episcopi potestate: ita accessus ad ipsum debet intelligi liber." For biographical details on Lapus Tactus see: Schulte *QL* vol. 2 p. 239. Note that although I have examined Lapus Tactus's *Lectura super Sexto* (Rome, 1589), I have not included an analysis of that work in this chapter. Like his contemporaries, Lapus Tactus chose to focus his brief gloss on matters of procedure—the rights of bishops with respect to *Periculoso*—and his commentary adds nothing significant to the conclusions arrived at in this chapter.

in fifteenth-century English commentary. A practical man, an active jurist, Petrus was influenced in his theoretical commentary by his dealings with the world. Petrus agreed with Joannes Andreae on virtually every significant point raised by *Periculoso*. He too stressed the importance of chastity for nuns, and found himself in complete agreement about the ways in which the Bonifacian legislation might be glossed to help preserve that virtue. Nevertheless, unlike Joannes, he had served as a government official and appears to have observed some of the resistance to enforcement of *Periculoso*—resistance that had merely been alluded to by his academic colleague. While difficulty of enforcement did not diminish Petrus's conviction that nuns should submit to the decree, it did convince him that they should have ample time to seriously consider such a course of action.

Dominicus de Sancto Geminiano, whose period of activity brings us into the fifteenth century, is the last influential canonist to be treated here. Born near Florence, he studied with Antonio de Butrio and became vicar of the bishop of Modena in 1407. He participated in the Synod of Pisa and then taught for some time at the University of Bologna. He subsequently became auditor of the Apostolic Chamber in Rome. He died before 1436.[33] Although Dominicus produced *consilia* and wrote on the *Decretum* and the Gregorian Decretals, his most important work was his *Lectura* on the *Liber Sextus*.[34]

When commenting on *Periculoso*, Dominicus de Sancto Geminiano relies heavily on Joannes Andreae, Joannes Monachus, and the Archdeacon. The form of his commentary, however, most closely follows that of Petrus de Ancarano. In two and one half folio pages Dominicus lists topics of significance—which by his time had become standardized—embedding within each citations from earlier commentary. He begins by noting (along with Joannes Andreae and Petrus de Ancarano) that although it is dangerous and detestable for nuns to go out of their monasteries, contrary custom which allows them to do so does

33. For the biography of Dominicus de Sancto Geminiano see: Smith, p. 88; Schulte, *QL* vol. 2 pp. 294–96.
34. I use the 1495 edition of this work, Hain # 7536: *Lectura super Sexto Decretalium cum notis Bernardini ex Capitaneis de Landriano* (Venetiis, per Baptistam de Tortis, 1495); hereafter cited as *Lectura*.

seem to exist. Such custom is not sound and healthy, and any custom leading souls into danger is not to be preserved.[35] Dominicus adduces the ruling of Pope Gregory the Great outlawing local customs which pose threats to the church as support for his position.[36]

Following Joannes Andreae *(GO* to *VI* 3.16.1 v.*spontanea)* he emphasizes that all nuns ought to assume their vows freely and not as a result of coercion, adding that to corrupt a nun so vowed is a grave offense that carries with it the opprobrium of God and of religion. He affirms *Periculoso*'s contention that to serve God freely one separates oneself from the active life and from the mundane, thus making contemplative existence more secure. Although stressing that a papal constitution binds all, everywhere, and interpreting Boniface VIII's wording in the sternest possible terms ("perpetual enclosure" means "for a lifetime"), Dominicus shows an awareness of the difficulties that those who sought to enforce such a drastic papal mandate might encounter. Having acknowledged already the existence of custom contrary to *Periculoso,* he now notes that ordinarily any new constitution imposing a harder state on a person would not include those persons already received into a community unless there was an express statement to that effect. Likewise, merely prohibiting those living under rules of enclosure from leaving their cloisters does not automatically prohibit others from entering. *Periculoso,* of course, *has* express statements on both of these points and so must be enforced as the peculiar, unequivocal legislation that it is.[37]

Dominicus defines *verecundia* as his predecessors had done, but in addition to patristic counsels he adds a quotation (allying innocence

35. *Lectura* to *VI* 3.16.1 v.*periculoso* "Nota primum quod periculosum est et detestabile moniales exire clausuras suorum monasteriorum et sic videtur quod licet consuetudo contrarium disponet, non tamen valeret, cum consuetudo inducens periculum animarum non sit servanda."

36. As cited in *X* 1.4.1, the rubric of which reads: "Consuetudines, quae ecclesiis gravamen inducere dignoscuntur, nostra nos decet consideratione remittere. . . ."

37. *Lectura* to *VI* 3.16.1 v.*periculoso* "Nota quod constitutio nova imponens duriorem statum personis non videtur includere personas iam receptas, nisi illud exprimatur in constitutione . . . Nota quod licet prohibitum existentibus sub clausura ut non exeant non tamen videtur prohibitum aliis ad alios habere accessum, nisi aliud exprimatur."

and modesty) from the orations of Seneca.[38] Questioning the right of abbesses to visit monasteries under their jurisdictions, Dominicus agrees with the Archdeacon that they must not have this right, since *Periculoso* speaks universally when it says "for whatever reason or cause," and what is said generally should be understood in general terms. Dominicus adds Joannes Andreae's observations that *Periculoso* has not been received in parts of Gaul and that it is also not accepted in Venice, but fails to comment upon this situation himself.[39] Responding to the question of whether an abbess might grant a special license to someone wishing to enter the cloister, Dominicus cites Joannes Monachus, who says no, since an abbess herself is bound by cloister regulations, and since, as the *Codex* noted, "women frequently act against their own best interests."[40]

When tackling the issue of the pope's right to obligate professed nuns to enclosure, that is, his right to impose a stricter rule of life than that under which the nuns entered, the *Lectura* takes a new turn. Joannes Monachus had argued that *Periculoso* really added nothing new to existing rules; Joannes Andreae argued that whatever was added had to be accepted, since monks and nuns, under obedience, had relinquished their own wills completely. Dominicus inclines toward Joannes Monachus's position. He contends that cloister regulations alone do not make for a harsher life; note, he says, the case of the Carthusian brothers, who, simply because they observe enclosure, cannot be said to have a stricter rule.[41]

38. Senecam declamatum, liber vii. The *Orationes,* which Seneca delivered in the senate or wrote for the Emperor Nero, are among his lost works. For the testimony of ancient authors regarding Seneca's lost works, and for fragments of those works, see L. Annaei Senecae, *Opera Que Supersunt,* ed. F. Haase.

39. *Lectura* to VI 3.16.1 v.*periculoso* "Sed nunquid liceat abbatisse exire monasterium pro visitandis monasteriis sibi subiecti? Solutio: Archidiaconus putat quod non; per istum textum sic universaliter loquentem dicendo 'quacumque ratione vel causa.' Unde oportebit quod faciat visitationem per alium. . . . Dicit tamen Joannes Andreae quod fertur istam consuetudinem non fuisse receptam in partibus gallicanis et dicit quod vidit ipsam etiam non servandam veneciis secundum eum."

40. Repeating the citation from the *Codex* 5.1.4 "Et mulieres ut plurimum adversus sua commoda laborare nituntur."

41. *Lectura* to VI 3.16.1 v.*periculoso:* "nota pro fratribus carthusiensibus: ex sola clausura continua non dicerent habere strictiorem regulam."

Next, Dominicus deals with the issue of admitting nuns into non-mendicant communities in excess of sustainable numbers. He confirms the right of the pope to invalidate vows taken in defiance of these restrictions and the fact that deceit, such as that evinced by Johannes de Deo's hypothetical question posed by virgins/penitents, is never permissible to circumvent them. He sounds a distinctly practical note when asking whether a novice who leaves a community before the end of her probation year should be held liable for reimbursing the community for the costs of her food and clothing. He concludes that the need for restitution cannot be demonstrated.[42]

The remainder of the *Lectura*'s treatment of *Periculoso* follows the *Glossa Ordinaria* closely. Dominicus affirms the unique right of the abbess to leave her cloister to render homage or fealty, provided she travel in suitable company, return promptly, and recognize that special dispensations cease to be effective when the circumstances that gave rise to them cease to exist.[43] He cites Roman law authority to support the case that women in general should not be compelled to appear in courts of law.[44] He refers the reader to Joannes Andreae's clarification of ordinary jurisdiction and the use of the secular arm in enforcing church law.[45] He also reproduces the hypothetical question, posed by Lapus Tactus: Could a bishop issue a constitution for an exempt monastery stating that none might enter save with his express consent? Could that same bishop, furthermore, decide whether someone had transgressed his decree and excommunicate them? Lapus, Dominicus reports, denies both points. While guarding the liberty of an exempt house, Dominicus does of course concede a bishop's prerogative of claustral supervision. It *would* be possible, Dominicus concludes, for a bishop to decree that no religious within his diocese, even if housed in an exempt monastery, act dishonorably.[46]

With the publication of Joannes Andreae's *Novella*, a second stage

42. *Lectura* to *VI* 3.16.1 v.*sane* "debeat restitituere alimenta monasterio . . . necessario hoc non probat."
43. Ibid. v.*verum*.   44. Ibid. v.*porro*.
45. Ibid. v.*Et quoniam*.
46. Ibid. "Secus aut esset si episcopus faceret constitutionem sub eadem pena vel alia quod nullus in tali monasterio in sua diocesi sito licet exempto aliquid inhonesti commitat."

of canonical comment on *Periculoso* had begun. The debt that the fourteenth-century canonists owed to the earlier glossators (and in the case of Joannes Andreae, the extent to which the *Novella* relied on his *Glossa Ordinaria*) was clear from the number of times influential predecessors such as Joannes Andreae and the Archdeacon were mentioned by name. Fundamental issues raised by the earliest commentators were seldom challenged and the opinions of these jurists were frequently reproduced verbatim. Earlier academic opinion, synthesized for the most part in the *Glossa Ordinaria,* was assumed to have settled the chief moral and theological questions suggested by *Periculoso*—questions such as the rationale for the strict cloistering of nuns and not of monks—and the fourteenth-century canonists felt free to turn their attention to more practical matters—to mechanics rather than morals.

In his *Novella,* Joannes Andreae confined his remarks about the nature of female chastity and the moral purpose served by claustration to single lines or sometimes single words, and usually referred his readers back to the *Glossa Ordinaria* or to the comments of the Archdeacon for further elaboration. Enforcement of *Periculoso* engaged him instead. He provided a practical solution for checking the delinquency of nuns in France and Venice—external visitation as set down by Clement V—and presented illustrations of specific actions (such as the reception of penitent prostitutes into an overcrowded community of nuns) that might undermine *Periculoso*'s intent. He was interested in clarifying, often in light of Roman law maxims, the terms of *Periculoso* and issues such as special licensing, ordinary jurisdiction, and the precise nature of the papal sanction for violators of the decree.

With Petrus de Ancarano, even the theological question of freedom of conscience among religious was dealt with pragmatically: an additional probationary year might increase the likelihood that nuns unused to enclosure would observe it. Like Joannes Andreae, Petrus concerned himself with clarifying the fine points of *Periculoso*—such as the extent of an ordinary's right over an exempt monastery—often using the Roman law to add both acuity and authority to his pronouncements.

Finally, Dominicus de Sancto Geminiano was so steeped in juristic reasoning that even when treating the subject of feminine frailty he preferred a citation from the *Codex* to a patristic reference. His mention of the Carthusian monks—an instance in which cloister for monks and nuns was more than theoretically equivalent—is made not to remind readers of the spiritual equality of monks and nuns but merely to prove that the pope had every right to impose strict enclosure on nuns, since cloister regulations alone did not imply a more onerous monastic rule. Like his contemporaries, Dominicus focused not on the important moral issues embedded in Boniface VIII's decree but rather on legal technicalities and practical matters of enforcement: the obligation to prefer church law over local custom, the expectation that a departing novice reimburse her community for expenses incurred on her behalf, the extent of an ordinary's jurisdiction in the performance of "extraordinary" duties.

Paralleling the difference between the "decretists" (the first commentators on Gratian's *Decretum*) and their successors, who commented on decretal legislation (the "decretalists"), the fourteenth-century canonists worked from a basis of previous accumulation and analysis. They were largely satisfied with what their predecessors, especially Joannes Andreae, had decided about the rationale for strict cloistering of nuns. The commentators seem to have been agreed that, save for specific orders like the aforementioned Carthusians, monks lived behind relatively permeable barriers created more by counsel than by canon. The commentators' task was simply to comment on legislation for nuns within a juristic rather than a moralistic framework. The fifteenth-century jurists, especially those who wrote treatises, would go even further in the direction of legal specificity.

S I X

Fifteenth-Century Commentary and Treatises

D
espite recurring outbreaks of the plague, war, and social un-
rest, legal scholarship continued to thrive in the fifteenth
century. Many new universities were founded in this period,
all offering instruction in either civil or canon law, with most schools
teaching both.[1] Although new universities sprang up in France and
Italy, nations with an already solid tradition of legal study, the greatest
expansion of higher education took place in Germany. Between 1364
and 1506 no fewer than fourteen new universities offering law degrees
were founded east of the Rhine.

Joannes Koelner de Vanckel was a product of this vibrant era in
German canonical scholarship. Master of liberal arts, doctor of both
laws, and ordinary professor of canon law at the University of Cologne,
Joannes flourished in the second half of the fifteenth century.[2] Several
fifteenth-century German editions of his *Summarium textuale et Conclusiones super Sexto, Clementinis* exist, testifying to the popularity of this

---

1. See Brundage, *Medieval Canon Law,* and Smith, *Medieval Law Teachers and
Writers,* chap. 9, for evidence of the concurrent teaching of civil and canon law
in the period.
2. Schulte *QL* vol. 2 p. 384; Van Hove, vol. 1 p. 501.

now obscure jurist's work for contemporaries.³ There was also an edition published in Paris in 1509.

Joannes devotes about two folio pages to his discussion of *Periculoso*. Following the form he uses throughout his *Summarium,* Joannes begins with a summary of the decree's provisions; then he draws his first of four conclusions: professed nuns throughout Europe ought to remain perpetually cloistered, neither leaving their enclosure nor allowing any to enter, save in exceptional cases.⁴ There follows a list of such exceptions. First, if a serious and infectious disease such as leprosy afflicts a nun, she threatens her sisters by staying within the cloister. Under such circumstances (as Boniface himself had clearly stated), she might be permitted to leave the confines of the monastery. Second, perpetual enclosure does not preclude the possibility that a nun might transfer to another order. Interestingly, Joannes does not contend that the transfer be made to a *stricter* order. Instead he merely cites a ruling from the *Clementines* about uniformity of religious habits and practice within any given community.⁵ Joannes's failure to enter into the discussion of his predecessors—canonists whose work he clearly knows and whose opinions he consistently cites—might imply a willingness to condone the transfer of professed nuns to communities less clearly affected by the strict enclosure regulations of *Periculoso.*

This observation is given added credibility by the next exception Joannes lists. *Periculoso,* he says, also does not bind those who live in regions in which it has not been received. In support, he cites Gratian's *dicta* (*ante* D. 4 c.4) stating that laws are instituted when they are pro-

3. Cologne editions, according to Schulte, appeared in 1483, 1488, 1493–94, and 1495. I have used the 1488 edition: *Summarium textuale et conclusiones super Sexto et Clementinis et summarium et effectus extravagantium Joannis XXII* (Coloniae: Johannes Koelhoff, 1488), cited hereafter as *Summarium.*

4. *Summarium* to *VI* 3.16.1 *prima conclusio* p.127 "Prima conclusio: Moniales professe ubicunque sint debent sub perpetua clausura permanere, nec possunt exire, aut alii illam intrare. Probature hic in &1 Et est vera regulariter; fallit in casibus hic positis."

5. Ibid. "si monialis laboraret tali morbo quod sine periculo aut scandalo infra clausuram stare non posset, ut si esset leprosa aut simili morbo infecta, ut hic in versic. 'nisi.' Secundo fallit secundum glossam in verbo 'perpetua' si vellit intrare aliam religionem . . . Idem si eligeretur ad regimen alterius monasterii, intellige eiusdem religionis et habitus iuxta *Clem* 1.3.1."

mulgated, but confirmed or made permanent only when they are approved by customary usage. He quotes Joannes Andreae's statement that *Periculoso* is not observed in parts of Gaul or in Venice to illustrate his point.[6]

"Reasonable and manifest cause" constitutes a final ground for breaking the general rule of strict enclosure mandated by Boniface VIII. Both adjectives, Joannes cautions, must apply when someone seeks to enter the cloister, and, in addition, a special license must be procured. For more information on who might grant such a license, and the arguments supporting the right of the papacy to impose a stricter rule on professed religious, Joannes refers his readers to the *Glossa Ordinaria*.[7] He then ends this section of the *Summarium textuale* by reiterating Joannes Andreae's teaching that, unlike seculars, those who live under a rule might have a stricter life imposed upon them by the pope, even against their wills. Unlike Joannes Andreae, he does not elaborate on this point and seems to adduce the statement merely to reaffirm the legitimacy of the papal mandate.[8]

In his second conclusion, Joannes poses the hypothetical case of a nun, gravely ill, who leaves her cloister without permission since the community's superior is unreachable. Would such unauthorized departure, he asks, be grounds for excommunication? Joannes agrees with Dom[inicus de Sancto Geminiano] that necessity obviates observing the letter of the law in this case. He also notes that in the text of *Periculoso* itself, there is no mention of a required license in cases of serious illness.[9]

6. Ibid. "Quarto posset dici quod cessaret hec constitutio, nec ligaret in illis partibus et locis ubi non est recepta, pro hoc": *Decretum* D. 4 d. p. c. 3 [which begins: "Leges instituntur, cum promulgantur, firmantur, cum moribus utentium approbantur."] . . . "et dicit Jo[annes] And[reae] quod fertur quod non fuit recepta in partibus gallicanis et vidit eam etiam Venetiis non observari."

7. Ibid. "Quinto possunt alii ingredi monasteria monialium quando subest rationabilis et manifest causa, que duo debent concurrere, et requiritur etiam ultra licentia specialis illius ad quem pertinet ut hic in versi. 'nulli que.' Et qui sunt tales persone vide hic in glo. verbi 'causa.' Et quomodo potuit papa monialibus strictiorem vitam imponere vide his in glos. 'verbi presentes.' "

8. Ibid. "Imo religiosis invitis potest districtior vita imponi per papam, non autem secularibus."

9. *Summarium* to *VI* 3.16.1 *secunda conclusio* p.128 "Possunt moniales gravi

Extraordinary circumstances might justify leaving a cloistered monastery without a special license, but, as Joannes contends in his third conclusion, permission to enter or exit must normally be given by a superior.[10] That superior, following Joannes Monachus, cannot possibly be the abbess, since she herself is bound by the strictures of enclosure. License to enter or exit must ordinarily be sought from the bishop.

Finally, Joannes follows precisely in the footsteps of his predecessors when he approves the limits that Boniface VIII placed on new admissions to cloistered communities.[11] This restriction applies only to nonmendicant communities and involves the ability of a house to sustain itself but not necessarily to do so in comfort, much less luxury. Attempts to bypass this part of *Periculoso*'s legislation by subterfuge, such as by using of tactics of John of God's "false prostitutes," are inexcusable.

As the form and content of Joannes Koelner's *Summarium textuale* illustrate, traditional commentaries on the decretals were still common. But along with the growth of new centers of legal learning, the fifteenth century witnessed the spread of new types of legal scholarship. The increasing technicality of the legal profession, as well as the profusion of legislative sources, occasioned the emergence of more specialized literature as well.

As mentioned earlier, the treatise *(tractatus),* while certainly not a new literary form, acquired new popularity in the fifteenth century.[12] A detailed analysis and exposition of some special topic of the law, the treatise served the needs of students and practitioners. Unlike the gloss

---

infirmate detrita, superiore absente de consensu, moniales exire superioris licentia non obtenta? Dom[inicus de Sancto Geminiano] tenet, in brevi superioris licentia haberi non possit et infirmitas est gravis et manifesta possit curari possit exire ad tempus donec curet et postea redire. Ad hoc & 'proxima' [referring to *Periculoso*] ubi exire abbatissa admittitur si pro alium homagium postulare non possit . . . Nec hoc loques infirmitatiae facet mentione de licentia. Ergo, non videt hoc casu necessaria, nec talis exientes liget, excommunicatione."

10. *Summarium* to *VI* 3.16.1 *tertia conclusio* p.128 "Ut quis possit intrare clausura monialium ex causa iusta aut moniales exire possint debet specialiter a superiori licentia eadem petita et obtenta." This superior cannot be the abbess since "secundum Jo[annem] Mo[nachem] ipsa ad clausuram artatur ergo contra eam non habet facere."

11. *Summarium* to *VI* 3.16.1 *ultima conclusio* p. 128.

12. See Smith, p. 17, and the introduction to this study.

or *apparatus,* treatises were not tied to any one text; they ranged freely over the canon law in an attempt to provide a thorough treatment of a single subject.

Although a few treatises dealing with the rules and regulations of monastic life exist, other subjects connected one suspects, with more lucrative areas of the law, seem to have exerted more of an appeal. A look at the index to the largest compilation of treatises for the period, the *Tractatus universi iuris,* shows that titles of interest to the generalist, wills or dowries for instance, and those geared to the requirements of the tax lawyer or procedural specialist, far outnumber titles relating to the religious life.[13] The ideas and concerns of *Periculoso* do surface, however, in the writing of three fifteenth-century canonists.

Raymundus Fraguier's treatise *De religiosis sectis eorumque auctoribus* reflects *Periculoso*'s bias in favor of traditional religious life for women, although it does not specifically cite that constitution.[14] Known to us today only as "a professor of law," Raymundus's personal obscurity is ironic, given the fact that his entire work is dedicated to attaching founders to the most famous religious orders of his day. He lists recognized male and female monastic orders from the early days of the Church through the pontificate of Pope Urban V (1362–1370), and attempts to explain how and when they were established.

In his list of recognized religious houses for women he includes those founded by St. Scholastica, the sister of St. Benedict, by St. Clare of Assisi, the Dominican sisters, and the penitent community, the Magdalenes of Blessed Jerome. In contrast, he condemns the Beguines, who live without a recognized rule, adducing Clement V's condemnations of the group.[15] He cites that same pope when concluding that both monks and nuns ought to be visited regularly by their ordinaries so that a high order of discipline might be maintained.[16]

13. *Tractatus universi iuris* 2nd. ed 22 vols. in 28 (Venice: Franciscus Zilettus, 1584–89).

14. Raymundus Fraguier, *De religiosis sectis eorumque auctoribus,* in *Tractatus universi iuris* vol. 14 f.103–105.

15. Raymundus Fraguier, *De religiosis . . .* f.105; "Beguardi et Beguinae inducta cuculla sine regula et obedientia quas damnat cle. ad nostra. de haere." He is citing Clement V's constitution, *ad nostram (Clem* 5.3.3).

16. Ibid. "Qualiter autem visitari debeant religiosae et moniales, traditur in clem. *attendentes (Clem* 3.10.2).

The work of another virtually anonymous canonist, Petrus de Perusio, also reflects the concerns expressed by Boniface VIII. In addition, it poses questions that illustrate the purely practical consequences of changes in status or location for professed female religious. Entitled *De mutatione status ecclesiarum,* Petrus de Perusio's treatise is concerned primarily with the economic ramifications of changes in position or rank among religious—women as well as men.[17] For instance, Petrus says that in Italy it is customary to give a free-will offering, commonly referred to as a dowry, at the time that a novice is received into a community. Should that money be relinquished by the monastery if the novice leaves before profession or if after profession she transfers to another house?[18]

In raising this issue of practical finance, Petrus recalls the earlier discussion of Dominicus de Sancto Geminiano. In glossing *Periculoso*'s limit on the number of nuns that a cloistered community could adequately sustain, Dominicus had asked whether a novice who left religion before the end of her probationary year should be held liable for reimbursing the community for the costs of her food and clothing.[19] Dominicus had found no precedent for such reimbursement, but Petrus de Perusio contends that the so-called dowry need not be relinquished by the monastery under any circumstances; he finds incontrovertible grounds for his conclusion: if the customary gift or dowry

---

17. Petrus de Perusio, *De mutatione status ecclesiarum,* in *Tractatus universi iuris* vol. 14 f.175–178.

18. Petrus de Perusio, *De mutatione* f.176 verso "Quinto principaliter quaeritur, de consuetudine quae in Italia est, quod licet de iure communi non possit recipi monachus in monasterio propter pecunium, quia tunc esset simonia . . . tamen est de more et consuetudine et tempore quod mulier in monialem recipitur vadit ad altare publicum, et ubi offert certam pecunia praesentem in remissionem peccatorum, vel dono ista pecunia Deo et beatae Mariae Virgini, iuxta vulgarem modum loquendi dicendo istam pecuniam esse dotum ipsius monialis: demum ista monialis probationis annum redit ad seculum, vel in primo monasterio profitetur, et postmodum transit legitime ad aliud monasterium an illa monialis recuperabit illam pecuniam a primo monasteria? Respondeo, non . . ." The gift, Petrus reasons, must be pure and unconditional otherwise the practice of giving such a "dowry" would be simoniacal.

19. See chap. 6, n. 42. For a discussion of monastic simony in an earlier period see: Joseph Lynch, *Simonical Entry into Religious Life from 1000–1260,* and chap. 2, n. 45 of this study.

was given with any conditions whatsoever, it might be construed as simoniacal. The Italian custom escapes the taint of simony only if it is a free, perfect, and irrevocable gift to the admitting community. Petrus's conclusion has special interest with respect to the further elaboration of judicial distinctions between monks and nuns, when we recall that all dowries, no matter how freely offered, had been banned in the case of monks since the mid thirteenth century.

When discussing the economic and juridical consequences of the destruction, extinction, or subdivision of female monastic communities, Petrus illustrates the power of the local ordinary—a principle embodied in Boniface VIII's constitution. If all of the nuns and the abbess of a monastery die, for example, the bishop is empowered to sell the property of the defunct monastery and put the proceeds to other pious uses, such as poor relief or the building of a church. Similarly, if a monastery with a large number of nuns is destroyed, a bishop may decide to split the membership into two different communities, providing equally, of course, for their economic solvency.[20]

Finally, Petrus clearly admits what earlier canonists had only obliquely referred to—while the cloister continued to be an important part of the monastic ideal, an element that theoretically stabilized the lives of monks as well as nuns, in fact, the lives of monks and nuns could be very different. Petrus states that monks simply have many more legitimate reasons to leave their cloisters. Not only the desire to transfer to another, stricter order but a call to the priesthood or to higher church office might absolve a monk from adhering to enclosure regulations.[21]

One late fifteenth-century treatise that cites *Periculoso* directly, and

20. Petrus de Perusio, *De mutatione* f.176 "quarto quaeritur si monasterium sit destructum et habebat magnam quantitatem monialium et episcopus unam partem illarum monialum [ad unum monasterium] et aliam partem transtulerit ad aliud monasterium, cui ex illis monasteriis acquirentur bona illius monasterii primi. . . ." Petrus raises several other questions dealing with the finances of nunneries in distress, highlighting the role of the local ordinary in each case.

21. Petrus de Perusio, *De mutatione* f.178 "sed monachus a claustro absolui non potest, nisi in casibus a iure concessis quaestione prima. Placuit casus autem concessi videntur isti, quod transeat ad arctiorem regulam, licet quando promovetur ad praelaturam suae vel alterius religionis. . . ."

refers to it repeatedly, is the work of the noted canonist and theologian Joannes Franciscus de Pavinis.[22] Named papal auditor by Pope Paul II (1464–71), Joannes worked in the papal curia until his death—sometime during the reign of Innocent VIII (1484–92). A doctor of both laws as well as a doctor of theology, Joannes wrote specialized legal treatises, such as his tracts on tithes and episcopal vacancies, as well as decretal commentaries. He also compiled collections of Roman Rota decisions.

Joannes's treatise *De visitatione episcoporum* is a comprehensive guide to diocesan visitation that mirrors the author's life-long interest in and service to canon law.[23] Twenty-two folio pages in length, it deals with questions of conduct among lay parishioners, secular clergy, monks, and nuns. In those portions of the treatise that deal with the visitation of female monasteries, a total of about two pages, the exacting principles set down in *Periculoso* dominate the text. Having determined both the desirability of annual monastic visitation and the rationale for it (correction and reformation), Joannes proposes a checklist for visitors to communities of women extracted, almost verbatim, from Clement V's decree *Attendentes*.[24] Visitors are to apply themselves diligently to assure that nuns not violate dress regulations by wearing silk, various furs, or sandals; that they not wear their hair long in a horn-shaped style nor put on striped and multicolored caps. They are to see to it that nuns do not attend dances, take part in secular banquets, and go walk-

---

22. See Schulte, *QL* vol. 2 pp. 331–33 for biographical and bibliographical details.

23. Joannes Franciscus de Pavinis, *De visitatione episcoporum*, in *Tractatus universi iuris* vol. 14 f.178–207.

24. Joannes Franciscus, *De visitatione* f. 182, #32 "Visitores autem huiusmodi sollicitudinis studium diligenter impendant, ut moniales ipsae pannis sericis, variorum fodraturis, sandalitiis, comatis, cornutis crinibus, scacatis et virgatis caputiolis non utantur, non choreas, non festa secularium prosequantur, non die noctuve per vicos et plateas incedant, aut voluptuosam alias vitam ducant, easque sollertius retrahant ab insolentias quibuslibet [sic], et mundi huius illecebras et inducant easdem ad impendendum in monasteriis suis devotum, et debitum virtutum domino famulatum, non obstantibus exemptionibus, et privilegiis quibuscumque, et in his compelli remediis opportunis et electas abbatissas inducere ad suscipiendam benedictionem infra annum a tempore confirmationis computandum, nisi subsit causa rationabilis, alias cadant a iure suo, ut plenius nota in *(Clem* 3.10.2 v.*Visitores)*."

ing through the streets and towns by day or night. Nuns must be warned to avoid all luxuriousness, and visitors are to gently guide them away from the allurements of the world and encourage them to concentrate on monastic devotion, compelling them to obey by all suitable measures, notwithstanding any privileges or exemptions that they may claim. Furthermore, anyone elected to the office of abbess should receive her blessing within a year of her confirmation, unless reasonable grounds for delay exist. If no grounds exist, but the delay does, the abbess-elect completely loses her right to office. In addition to those aspects of monastic discipline cited by Pope Clement V, visitors are to pay attention to everything set out in Boniface VIII's decree *Periculoso;* that is to say, everything having to do with enclosure of nuns. Of these stipulations Joannes specifically mentions numerical restrictions on nonmendicant communities and *Periculoso*'s stipulations concerning a nun's performance of homage or fealty or her conduct of business in secular courts.[25]

Designed as a comprehensive guide, *De visitatione episcoporum* sets down behavioral prescriptions for visitors as well as for the religious they are empowered to correct. For example, Joannes discusses what visitors should expect to eat or drink during their stay within monastic precincts. He adduces Clement V's decree condemning some prelates who, ministering to the Cistercians, demanded that they be given meat at their meals—a food forbidden the monks by their rule.[26] He advises that all visitors be content with the ordinary daily fare of a given monastery, or that they supplement that provision by soliciting meals from households in the vicinity. This is especially true, he adds, when visits are made to communities of women, since all, tacitly or expressly professed, in those monasteries are bound by cloister regulations. Paraphrasing *Periculoso* he goes on to delineate precisely what those regulations imply: inability to leave the monastery save for grave, com-

---

25. Joannes Franciscus, *De visitatione* f. 182, #33 "Debet etiam talis visitator attendere omnia quae habentur in causa i de sta. regul. Liber VI videlicet circa clausuram monialium, et quod ultra facultates monasteriorum non mendicantium nulla recipiatur et quomodo fieri debeat homagium et fidelitas dominis temporalibus et secularibus, et quid agendum quando in ecclesiastico vel seculari foro causas habent. . . ."

26. Joannes Franciscus, *De visitatione* f. 184, using the terms of *Clem* 3.13.2.

municable illness, and restricted entrance to the cloister, save with special license. By implication, the resources of cloistered communities would (and *should*) be inadequate for more than spartan hospitality.[27]

When commenting on the jurisdiction and obligations of the ordinary, Joannes again refers to *Periculoso* almost word for word. If a monastery of nuns is not enclosed, the ordinary should procure through pious donations the needed resources to sustain that community. When he has done so, the nuns are to be strictly cloistered, and those who refuse to conform to such restrictions censured by the Church, which may invoke the secular arm when needed.[28] Joannes also touches on aspects of female enclosure when he sets down guidelines for the visitation of monks. Visitors should make sure that monks guard against incautious relations with nuns, that they not remain in the nun's monasteries, nor carry on long conversations with nuns, even if they are relatives. A few words, exchanged only in the presence of the abbess, should suffice.[29] Finally, Joannes advises visitors to issue

27. Ibid. "maxime cum visitantur monasteria monialium, vel hospitalia, quoniam tales sub perpetua in suis monasteriis clausura teneri debent cum sunt expresse vel tacite professe, nisi propter morbum aliquem non posset cum aliis absque gravi periculo, seu scandalo commorari, et nulli maxime inhoneste personae, nisi rationibus et manifesta causa existat, absque illius, ad quem pertinuerit specialis licentia ingressus, vel accessus ad eas patere debet, ut sint a publicis et mundanis aspectibus separatae et omnino Deo servire valeant liberius et lasciviendi opportunitate sublata eisdem corda sua et corpora in omni sanctimonia diligentius custodire."

28. Joannes Franciscus, *De visitatione* f.184, #19 ". . . abbates vero et alii tam exempti quam non exempti praelati ecclesiarum monasteriorum et ordinum quorumcunque in monasteriis huiusmodi sibi subiectis, de clausura convenienti, ubi non est, ipsorum monasteriorum expensis et fidelium eleemosynis, quas ad hoc procurent, diligentius facienda, et de ipsis monialibus includendis, quam primum commode poterunt providere procurent, contradictores atque rebelles per censuram ecclesiasticam appellatione postposita compescendo, invocato ad hoc, si opus fuerit, auxilio brachii secularis . . ."

29. Joannes Franciscus, *De visitatione* f.204, # 52 and 53 "ut patet quod monacho convivari cum monacha, nec secum in eodem monasterio manere, nec loqui, etiam cum consanguinea, nisi per verba compendiosa, ita quod cito recedat, et sub testimonio abbatissae et idem de abbate . . ."; also, f.207 verso, #20 "nec monachi ad eas accedere debent, nec econtra: nec cum eis colloqui, nisi in praesentia abbatissae, et per modica verba . . ."

a general caution to people in the vicinity of a cloistered monastery: not even respectable persons of one sex should enter the cloister of another, save for manifest and reasonable cause (such as in the case of physicians, barbers, carpenters, dressmakers, and the like), without a special license. To validate his warning, he quotes again from *Periculoso:* cloister restrictions apply so that "nuns may be able to serve God more freely, wholly separated from the public and worldly gaze and, occasions for lasciviousness having been removed, they may most diligently safeguard their hearts and bodies in complete chastity."[30]

The publication of Joannes Andreae's *Novella* marked the beginning of a more pragmatic, juridically oriented commentary, and fifteenth-century canonists writing on *Periculoso* continued that trend. Building on, and making specific reference to, the work of noted predecessors such as Joannes Andreae, Joannes Monachus, and Dominicus de Sancto Geminiano, these canonists dealt even more exhaustively with the technicalities surrounding the enforcement and possible evasion of strict claustration. Above all, their work illustrated the trend toward further elaboration of the juridical differences between monks and nuns. Petrus de Perusio dealt almost exclusively with matters of finance as they affected cloistered communities; he showed his debt to earlier jurists by trying to resolve issues they posed—specifically, by addressing the questions raised by Dominicus de Sancto Geminiano. He pointed up the differences between monks and nuns by stressing the power of the ordinary over the fiscal affairs of women's houses as well as by noting the continued practice of endowing women, but not men, upon profession. Joannes Franciscus de Pavinis left detailed instructions for bishops visiting monastic communities of women. In addition to reiterating and expanding upon the strict cloister regulations set down in *Periculoso,* Joannes illustrated just what sort of result en-

---

30. Joannes Franciscus, *De visitatione* f.206, #19 "Monendus est populus, ut caveat ab ingressu monasteriorum nam nulli etiam honestae personae, nisi rationabilis et manifesta causa existat, sicut in medicis, barbitonsoribus, carpentariis, sartoribus, et aliis similibus, sine speciali licentia illius ad quem pertinet ingredi monasteria mulierum, nec econtra mulieribus virorum, ut sic a publiciis et mundanis conspectibus separatae omnino servire Deo valeant liberius et lasciviendi opportunitate sublata eisdem corda sua et corpora in omni sanctimonia diligentius custodire."

forcement of those rules might have when he cautioned visitors to nunneries to expect nothing more than spartan fare.

Only one of the fifteenth-century canonists studied, Joannes Koelner de Vanckel, appeared to be willing to countenance a loosening of the strictures imposed by Boniface VIII. Joannes detailed permissible exceptions to *Periculoso,* including the transfer of a nun to another order. Indeed, by observing that a law does not bind those who live in a region in which it has not been received (i.e. *Periculoso* in parts of France and in Venice, according to Joannes Andreae), Joannes might have developed an argument designed to seriously limit the effectiveness of *Periculoso*—and papal legislation as a whole. Yet, like Joannes Andreae before him, Joannes Koelner did not pursue this tack. Instead he counterbalanced his observation by insisting that under normal circumstances every exit from, or entrance into, a cloistered community be accompanied by the requisite license, and by supporting Joannes Andreae's position regarding the relative rightlessness of nuns faced with the imposition of a rule of life harsher than that under which they were professed.

Of all the fifteenth-century commentaries, Joannes Franciscus de Pavinis's *De visitatione episcoporum* is perhaps the best example of the way in which academics tried to make *Periculoso* a real part of ecclesiatical practice. Joannes paraphrased or quoted directly from *Periculoso* whenever aspects of cloister regulation were at issue. He attempted to transform a sweeping mandate into a means of regular discipline and/ or reformation.

S E V E N

English Canonists—Independent but Allied Traditions

As in Germany, so also in England, the late Middle Ages was a boom period for the study of canon law. Spurred on by criticism of clerical ignorance of the law, universities such as Oxford and Cambridge were increasingly called upon to educate diocesan officials. The teaching and study of canon law flourished in late fourteenth-century England, continuing apace until royal decrees, such as the one that terminated the Cambridge canon law faculty in 1535, restricted ecclesiastical jurisdiction.[1]

The course of study for would-be English canonists replicated the continental curriculum. It required a preliminary study of the Roman law and a thorough knowledge of Gratian's *Decretum* and subsequent

1. Dorothy M. Owen, *The Medieval Canon Law,* pp. 1–2; see also Richard Helmholz, *Roman Canon Law in Reformation England,* and F. Donald Logan, "The First Royal Visitation of the English Universities, 1535," with reference to the end of university instruction at Cambridge and Oxford during the English Reformation. On the canon law curricula, see Leonard E. Boyle, "The Curriculum of the Faculty of Canon Law at Oxford in the First Half of the Fourteenth Century," and James A. Brundage, "The Cambridge Faculty of Canon Law and the Ecclesiastical Courts of Ely."

decretal collections. In addition, however, legatine and synodal legislation peculiar to England was also part of the English law student's curriculum.

The two most prominent English canonists of the late Middle Ages, John Acton and William Lyndwood, wrote glosses on thirteenth-century legatine or episcopal statutes which amplified papal legislation in view of specific English needs. Both Acton and Lyndwood grafted papal constitutions, including *Periculoso,* onto existing provincial legislation, thus pointing up both the importance of such law to the English canonical tradition and the gulf between continental theory and national practice.

John Acton (alternately spelled Athon or Ayton) was a graduate of Cambridge and canon of Lincoln.[2] While in the service of the archbishop of Canterbury from 1333 to 1348, he wrote a commentary on the constitutions of two papal legates, Otto (1237) and Ottobuono (1268). Entitled *Constitutiones legitime seu legatine regionis anglicane,* his gloss survived in numerous manuscripts and was later incorporated into printed editions of the work of his even more famous successor, William Lyndwood.[3]

John Acton's comments on *Periculoso* are framed by a legatine statute of Cardinal Ottobuono—the papal legate whose staff included the young Benedict Caetani![4] Issued under the rubric *Quod moniales certa loca non exeant,* statute 52 of the Legatine Council of St. Paul's London, summoned by Ottobuono in April 1268, deals with the strict enclosure of nuns.[5]

Ottobuono stated that, having renounced the world for the perpet-

2. For biographical detail see: C. R. Cheney, "Legislation of the Medieval English Church," pp. 193, 217; Owen, *The Medieval Canon Law,* p. 2.

3. I have used the 1504 edition (Paris: Johannes Confluentinus) of John Acton's *Constitutiones,* as it will be cited hereafter; the 1679 edition (Oxford) of Lyndwood's *Provinciale* includes the legatine canons with Acton's gloss.

4. The future Pope Boniface VIII had been in Ottobuono's service since 1266 according to T. S. R. Boase, *Boniface VIII,* pp. 11–13; see chap. 4 of this study for the implications of this "English connection" with respect to *Periculoso.*

5. For details concerning the composition of the council, as well as for the text of the statute see: *Councils & Synods with other documents relating to the English church,* part 2, pp. 738–39 and 789–91.

ual service of Christ, nuns should guard their senses from evil desires and malign influences. In order that they preserve their innocence of mind and body, they must not be allowed to leave their monasteries. They could enter their chapel, chapter house, dormitory, and refectory at the appointed times, for prayer, correction, and refreshment of the body respectively. At other hours they were to remain within their cloister contemplating God, receiving through that earnest meditation a foretaste of heaven.

The cloistered precincts were to be strictly off limits to seculars save only infrequently and for just cause. Nuns were not to speak to any man, or indeed any person, religious or secular, except in public. At least one other nun was to be present at such meetings and the content of the conversation was to be serious. Confessions were, of course, excepted. Nuns were not to eat meals outside the cloister save with permission of their superiors and then only in the company of a relative or some person completely above suspicion. All other places beyond those specified above were to be completely forbidden to nuns, with the exception of the infirmary or other place in which an ailing nun might, with permission of her abbess or prioress, recoup her strength.

Only obedientiaries—sisters charged with administrative duties, such as oversight of the infirmary or kitchen—were to perform duties that took them outside of the monastery, and then only with suitable companions. Indeed, abbesses and prioresses themselves were not to leave the monastery save for urgent necessity or evident advantage, and then always with upright company. Their inferiors were never to be granted licenses to leave the monastery, except for just or necessary cause and in the company of another nun. Finally, Ottobuono declared that nuns were not to take part in public processions but to hold their processions within their monastic precincts. He concluded by enjoining those archbishops, bishops, and other prelates who had jurisdiction over female religious houses (and upon whom the burden of visitation fell) to cause his statutes to be strictly observed. John Acton reproduces the text of statute 52 in full. He then interjects, at every opportunity, mention of more recent papal legislation that in his view reinforces Ottobuono's efforts. Chief among these papal enactments is *Periculoso*.

To clarify the use of the term *moniales,* Acton says, there are ample sources to adduce, including *Periculoso* and the decree of Clement V, *Attendentes.*[6] So too, if the reader requires additional illustration of the use of the term *perpetuo* as it applies to the cloistered life of nuns, he is referred to Boniface VIII's constitution.[7] *Periculoso* is cited to expand upon Ottobuono's cautions regarding the "honest society" in which a nun, required to leave her monastery, was to travel. It is also used to underscore the idea that nuns were simply never to casually enjoy this privilege.[8]

Having used citations from subsequent papal legislation in the most conventional manner, and having interpreted Ottobuono's decree in strict terms, Acton reserves his less inhibited, and much more telling, comments for the last. Ottobuono had concluded canon 52 by enjoining ordinaries to "cause his statutes to be strictly observed"—an injunction that Acton sees as anything but simple to execute:

> but surely, since scarely any mortal man could do this, we must understand these words to mean "as far as they are able to," for the nuns respond to these statutes, or to others concerning their lasciviousness saying that those who made those laws were putting much confidence in their own highmindedness when they burdened them with these hard and intolerable restrictions. We see that these statutes are never, or badly, observed and so we might ask why the holy fathers bothered to labor so hard only to "beat the air."[9]

No pessimist, Acton refuses to allow difficulty of enforcement to spell defeat. The work of "the holy fathers" is meritorious, he con-

---

6. *Constitutiones* f.cxix verso ad v. *moniales* "hic addiciit pleniorum tractatus ad hoc, id est de sta. reg. periculoso li.vi et clem. ti. attendentes."

7. *Constitutiones* f.cxix verso ad v. *perpetuo* ". . . exponit de sta. reg. periculoso . . ."

8. *Constitutiones* f.cxix recto ad v. *moniales alia* and f.cxx verso ad v. *monasteria non exeant.*

9. *Constitutiones* f.cxx recto ad v. *faciant observari;* "sed certe vix hoc faceret homo mortalis, ideo subaudiendum est hic quatenus id eis est . . . respondent moniales statutis istis vel aliis contra earumque lascinias editis quorum valde fidebant tales statuentes in conscientiis suis quando talia ordinauerunt pro suas arctationes sic intolerabiliter duras. unde ad oculos videmus hec statuta vel in nullo vel male observari. ut quid ergo sancti patres isti sic laborando aerem verbetaverunt."

cludes, since we look not to what is, but to what, in justice, should be ("non ergo aspicimus ad id quod sit sed ad illud quod de iure fieri convenit"). To provide precedent for his idealism, Acton cites a very appropriate passage from St. Bernard of Clairvaux's *On Consideration*— a tract dedicated to reminding the encumbered bureaucrat, Pope Eugenius III, of his pastoral duties.[10] In Book IV, chapter two of *On Consideration*, Bernard tells the pope not to despair, even if it appears that the intractable Roman people will never be cured of their evils. Scripture requires a pastor to care for, but not neccesarily to cure, his flock. Eugenius should remember the words of St. Paul (1 Cor. 15.10) "I labored more than all," *not*, "I did more good than all" or "I bore more fruit than all." Glory more in labor than in success, St. Bernard adds. Plant, water, and tend, and you have done your part; only God can decide when and if he will give increase.

In sum, although Acton demonstrates that he is aware of the reality of the situation in English female monasteries, he blames the clergy for the laxity with which strict enclosure rules are enforced. In spite of the recognized difficulty of their task, he upbraids prelates for negligence, and observes that growing contumacy might be aptly treated by increased penalties for infraction.[11] While *Periculoso* is not adduced to reinforce that final point, Acton certainly had its concluding injunctions to ordinaries in mind—injunctions that surpassed those of Ottobuono in their rigor.

Another even more influential English canonist, William Lyndwood, codified English synodal legislation, as constituted by successive archbishops of Canterbury, in a massive work called the *Provinciale seu Constitutiones Anglie*.[12] Born about 1375, Lyndwood (whose name appears variously as Lyndewode, Lindewood, and Lindwood) was

10. Ibid. The following paraphrase is based on the translation of St. Bernard, *Five Books On Consideration*, trans. J. Anderson and E. Kennan. For the Latin text see St. Bernard, *Opera*, ed. J. LeClercq, C. H.Talbot, H. M. Rochais, et al.

11. Ibid. ". . . in quibus crescente contumacia crescere debet est pena."

12. For biographical details as well as a full history of the manuscript and print tradition of the *Provinciale* see: *DNB* vol. 12 pp. 340–42; see also the analysis of content in C. R. Cheney, "William Lyndwood's Provinciale," pp. 405–34.

educated at Gonville and Pembroke halls, Cambridge, and received his law degree from Oxford. In 1414 he became chancellor of the archbishop of Canterbury, Henry Chichele—a situation that gave him ample practical experience in the English canon law, since he also served as official of the archbishop's court. Lyndwood completed the *Provinciale* in the busy years 1422–30; late in life, he became bishop of St. Davids. He died in 1446.

Beginning with the constitutions of Archbishop Stephen Langton and ending with those of his master, Henry Chichele, the *Provinciale* accompanied the text of each archiepiscopal statute with a gloss. Since many statutes had previously been in a state of disorder, hard to find or interpret, and thus neglected, Lyndwood aimed to produce a useful tool for prelates and judges.[13] Immensely popular, Lyndwood's work "remained the leading authority on the English ecclesiastical law right through the period of the Reformation, the legal textbook which was probably most often consulted by the middle and lower ranks of the ecclesiastical legal profession."[14]

Like John Acton, Lyndwood treats *Periculoso* in conjunction with the specifically English material that is his subject matter. Reference is made to *Periculoso* when Lyndwood glosses three statutes—two attributed to Stephen Langton and one to John Pecham. Since the *Provinciale* arranged the archiepiscopal statutes under titles modeled on those of the books of the decretals, all relevant comment occurs in Book III, under the title *de statu regularium*.

The first explicit reference to *Periculoso* occurs in Lyndwood's gloss of a canon of Archbishop Stephen Langton promulgated at the Council of Oxford in 1222. *Incipit* notwithstanding, the canon—*Inhibemus ne*

13. Cheney, ibid., p. 407; note also Cheney's comment on page 426 that if Lyndwood "occasionally took liberties with his texts, he seldom perverted the sense seriously."

14. Ralph Houlbrooke, *Church Courts and the People during the English Reformation 1520–70*, p. 19; the *Provinciale* was one of the first lawbooks to be printed anywhere in England. Cheney gives a concise history of the most important editions on pp. 430–34; I have used the 1501 edition: *Provinciale seu Constitutiones Anglie. Cum summariis atque iustis annotationibus, honestis characteribus, summaque accuratione rursum expresse* (Paris: A. Bocard, 1501), cited hereafter as *Provinciale*.

moniales—concerned religious men as well as women.[15] Save with episcopal consent, *Inhibemus ne moniales* forbade nuns to receive any secular women within the walls of their monasteries, necessary servants
excepted. It required the license of a superior anytime nuns *or monks*
wished to leave their houses, specifying that such permission not be
given without just cause and that a license contain an appointed
homecoming date. As a remedy for delinquency, Langton allowed ordinaries to place an offender in another monastery of the same order
until he fully repented his fault.

Even before Lyndwood actually cites *Periculoso* as a supporting text,
his gloss of *Inhibemus ne moniales* reflects a thorough acquaintance with
both the constitution and its commentary. For instance, Lyndwood
notes that the term *moniales* includes the abbess, an observation that
echoes the opinions of nearly all of *Periculoso*'s continental glossators.[16]
Aware that *Inhibemus ne moniales* is very different from *Periculoso*, in that
it clearly states that neither monks nor nuns should leave their monastic precincts without license of their superiors, Lyndwood nevertheless alleges *Periculoso*, as well as Ottobuono's statute 52, when he
glosses the word *egredi*.[17] Saying that all these rulings on religious enclosure contain "similar" directives, he does not seem to be bothered
by the gender-specific nature of Boniface VIII's constitution. His single
additional citation of *Periculoso* for this canon occurs at the words *scepta
domus:* "today all nuns ought to be enclosed, nor should they leave [the
cloister precincts]."[18]

Omnem autem singularitatem, another of Stephen Langton's canons,
covered a variety of issues affecting monastic discipline. After ruling
out all "singularity" in dining and dress among religious men and

15. *Provinciale* f. cxiii; A good English translation of the text of all *Provinciale*
canons is *Lyndwood's Provinciale*, ed. J. V. Bullard and H. Chalmer Bell; *Inhibemus
ne moniale* is found on pp. 83–84.
16. Recall the lengthy discussion in Joannes Andreae's *Novella* ad v.*partibus*
as well as mention of the subject by Dominicus de Sancto Geminiano and
Joannes Koelner de Vanckel.
17. *Provinciale* f. cxiii ad v. *egredi* "simile habes in constitutione Octoboni
moniales et eodem ti. c. unico li. vi."
18. *Provinciale* f. cxiii ad v. *scepta domus* "hodie deberent omnes moniales
recludi ne exeant sicut legitur eodem ti. c. unico li. vi."

women, Langton urged bishops to provide specifically for nuns: "Let the bishops also provide that nuns may be sustained in all things necessary with the goods of their monastery and suffer none to be admitted above their number, or any to be received after they be once brought to their number."[19] Langton further called for the deposition of any abbess or prioress who allowed admissions contrary to his ordinance.

It is this segment of *Omnem autem singularitatem* that Lyndwood sees as directly parallel to Boniface VIII's stipulations about the maximum number of nuns allowable in nonmendicant communities. Once again he shows himself an informed student of continental commentary, since in clarifying the words "all things necessary" he cites the Archdeacon's gloss to *Periculoso*.[20] He adds a refinement to the words "be sustained" by noting that *Periculoso* stipulates that such support (save in mendicant communities) obviate penury.[21] Finally, Lyndwood mentions that while *Omnem autem singularitatem* provides for the deposition of a refractory head of a female house, *Periculoso* makes it clear that any admissions over and above the prescribed numbers for that house are to be declared void.[22]

Lyndwood makes the most thorough use of *Periculoso,* and comments most extensively on the difficulties surrounding its enforcement when glossing a canon attributed to Archbishop John Pecham. *Sanctimoniales* was promulgated by Pecham at or shortly before the Council of Lambeth in 1281.[23] It is concerned exclusively with nuns and their freedom to leave their monasteries and is worth quoting in full:

> Many nuns who delight in the vice of wandering, following the example of the wandering Dinah, continually fall into a similar or rather a more pernicious scandal of corruption. We, watchful against this dan-

19. Translated in *Lyndwood's Provinciale,* ed. Bullard and Bell, pp. 84–85.
20. *Provinciale* f. cxv ad v. *omnibus necessariis* "nota Archi[diaconus] v. necessaria li. vi."
21. *Provinciale* f. cxv ad v. *sustenari* "sine penuria, eodem ti. c. unico & sane li. vi. quo ad ordines non mendicantium."
22. *Provinciale* f. cxv ad v. *deponatur* "de iure communi pena est quod talis receptio non tenet, eodem ti. c. unico & sane li. vi."
23. *Councils and Synods,* ed. Powicke and Cheney, pp. 886–87; for the Latin text of the canon see pp. 911–12.

ger, wishing to look after their health rather than to please their vain desires, forbid under pain of excommunication any of them, either alone or in company, to stay with their parents or kin, however closely related, or with strangers, however highly esteemed or religious, over and above the three days normally accorded for purposes of recreation, nor, for any other necessary cause or occasion (sickness only excepted) over and above six days, save when it pleases local bishops, whose consciences we burden with the thought of the final judgment. This ordinance we do not extend, however, to those compelled to go outside to beg for their necessities of life, while they are begging.[24]

Lyndwood begins his gloss of *Sanctimoniales* by stating that, although all religious are prohibited from wandering, nuns are especially constrained, as both *Periculoso* and Clement V's *Attendentes* attest.[25] Lyndwood makes sure that his readers recall that Dinah, daughter of Jacob, on her way to visit the women of the region, was raped by Shechem, son of Hamor, the local ruler.[26] He then explains, following a hallowed patristic tradition, that Pecham's reference to ''a more pernicious corruption'' reflects the fact that Dinah's sin was one of simple fornication, while a nun's corruption, in view of her marriage to Christ, would be adultery.[27]

24. The Latin reads as follows: ''Sanctimoniales plurime in vagationis vitio delectate, Dyne vagantis exemplo, in consimile corruptionis scandalum immo longe perniciosius assidue prolabuntur. Cui periculo providentes, magis optantes earum saluti consulere quam vanis earundem desideriis complacere, sub pena excommunicationis totaliter inhibemus ne qua illarum etiam cum socia, nedum sola, apud parentes vel affines quantumcunque propinquos, nedum apud extraneos quantumcunque fame, eminentie, vel religionis existant, ultra tres dies naturales causa recreationis perhendinare, seu pro quacunque necessitate vel occasione ultra sex dies, cessante infirmitate, commorari presumant; nisi locorum episcopis aliud aliquotiens ex causa necessaria videatur, de quo eorum conscientias in tremendo iudicio oneramus. Hanc autem ordinationem ad illas non extendimus que exterius coguntur mendicare sibi necessaria, dum mendicant.''

25. *Provinciale* f. cxvi ad v. *vagationis* ''quibus personis religiosis prohibetur . . . maxime monialibus sicut periculoso eodem ti. li. vi. et c. attendentes in clem.''

26. *Provinciale* f. cxvi ad v. *Dyne* ''filia Jacob,'' citing Genesis 34 for the story.

27. *Provinciale* f. cxvi ad v. *longe perniciosius* ''non erat simplex fornicatio . . . sed in corruptione monialis non solum commitur fornicatio sed adulterium quod sponsa Christi . . .''

There follows a lengthy section in which Lyndwood relies almost exclusively on *Periculoso* to clarify and to intensify Pecham's ordinance.[28] When required to leave their cloisters, he says, nuns are to have decent and honest companions. They are, moreover, to remain perpetually enclosed except in two cases: grave and evident disease that might endanger the lives of other community members, and the need of an abbess to perform homage or fealty. Both the constitution of Pecham, Lyndwood continues, and the later ruling of Boniface VIII should have the force of law, yet *Periculoso* is not fully accepted in England. While efforts to enforce it at first proceeded apace, doubts began to be raised about whether nuns could be compelled to be perpetually cloistered in the manner prescribed by Boniface. Lyndwood concludes that the failure of many English houses to abide by the regulations of *Periculoso* can be explained by the tepidity of bishops who, it is implied, allowed themselves to be swayed by those doubts. To confirm his conclusion, Lyndwood mentions the fact that houses subject to monastic superiors have fared far better; in fact, the majority of those nunneries *have* become cloistered, whereas those communities under immediate episcopal supervision remain unenclosed.

28. *Provinciale* f. cxvi ad v. *cum socia* ". . . monasterium exire non debet nisi cum honesta et decenti societate, sicut eodem ti. li vi. et non nisi ex certa causa . . . moniales remanere debent sub perpetua claustra nec exire debent quovismodo nisi in duobus casibus. . . . infirmitas evidens . . . propter quod non possit sine gravi periculo seu scandalo morari cum aliis in monasterio . . . secundus casus abbatissam vel priorissam exire cum homagia facienda . . . Et propterea constitutio ista modicum vim obtinet respectu iuris communis quod tolli non potest per constitutionem inferioris . . . Si igitur quiras de quo operat ista constitutio maxime cum Jo. Peccham auctor huius constitutionis bene noverat constitutionem illam bonifacianam eodem ti. li. vi.*[Periculoso]* Responsionem bonam non video nisi quod illa constitutio Bonifacii forsan non erat acceptata in anglia nec executa prout in pluribus monasteriis monialium in anglia hodie videmus ad oculos. Verum in hoc casu bene precedit ista constitutio quod disponit circa ipsarum egressum. Sed tunc insurgit dubium quomodo possent moniales resistere huiusmodi constitutioni praedicte: ut semper non remaneant iste incluse . . . Sed verum est in regno anglie pro maiori parte quod moniales quae reguntur per religiosos sunt incluse. Ille vero quae immediate subsunt episcopo non sunt incluse et sic apparet quod negligentia circa hoc remansit in episcopis nec potest contra illud ius prescribi prout ibi nota Archidiaconus supra verbum obedientie [citing Guido de Baysio] Et sic prescriptio episcopos excusare non potest."

There is no ambiguity in William Lyndwood's description of the fate of *Periculoso,* and his alleged reasons for that fate. Like John Acton a century before him, Lyndwood concluded his discussion of cloister regulations by ascribing blame for their haphazard application to the ordinaries. Candidly admitting the failures of the English bishops to carry out archiepiscopal and even papal mandates, he nevertheless idealistically (again recalling Acton) insisted on renewed action. According to Boniface VIII, bishops were directed to oversee the enclosure of all female religious within their jurisdictions—it was up to the bishops to fulfill their responsibilites, and to do so as soon as possible.

John Acton, and William Lyndwood a century later, both concluded that many English nuns did not abide by strict enclosure regulations. Both blamed English bishops for the lapse in discipline. But was the blame leveled correctly? Did bishops shirk their duties, or did they attempt to comply with Boniface VIII's decree to enclose all female religious within their jurisdictions? If they did try to enforce *Periculoso,* why did they fail? A glance at the recording of other scholars, in particular the wealth of data appended to Eileen Power's classic study of medieval English nuns, provides some tentative answers to those important questions.

Bishops' registers are the single most valuable source of evidence about episcopal enforcement of *Periculoso* in England. Not only do they record the activities of bishops as they visited and corrected monastic communities, but by the fourteenth century they sometimes include records of the bishop's court of audience as well.[29] Audience courts often dealt with corrections arising from visitation presentments. The English ecclesiastical court system was a many-tiered operation, with considerable jurisdictional overlap. The enforcement of *Periculoso* raises issues that would most likely have been handled in the audience court, by the bishop personally or by his delegated official.[30]

29. Dorothy M. Owen, "An Episcopal Audience Court," pp. 140–49; the published register of Bishop Martival of Salisbury 1315–29, treated in this chapter, provides an example of an audience court act book appended to an episcopal register.

30. Owen, "An Episcopal Audience Court" pp. 141 and 144. For pertinent discussions of English ecclesiastical jurisdiction see Charles Donahue, "Why

Episcopal register entries dating from the time that *Periculoso* first appeared in England demonstrate that bishops did attempt to require the nuns in their dioceses to comply with Boniface VIII's decree. One of the earliest of these efforts was made by Simon of Ghent, bishop of Salisbury. In 1299 he sent a long letter to the abbess of Wilton, enjoining the Benedictine nuns of that house to obey *Periculoso*.[31] The letter begins with the full text of the constitution and ends with a precise statement regarding its implementation: From this time forward, the nuns of Wilton are to regulate their comings and goings, their admission of seculars, and their reception of new sisters by the words of *Periculoso;* walls are necessary to the proper application of cloister regulations and the nuns are to have the walls around their house properly built and maintained. If, for some valid reason, this task proves impossible to accomplish within the prescribed time limits, the bishop requires them to notify him within eight days of the Feast of the Purification. The bishop concludes with a statement of the spirtitual rationale for such strict regulation. Your heavenly Spouse, he tells them, for love of you, will so spark your desires that the terrestrial will seem bitter and seclusion from all occasions of worldly pleasure sweet.[32] In

---

the History of Canon Law Is Not Written," pp. 20–21; Ralph Houlbrooke, *Church Courts and the People During the English Reformation 1520–1570,* pp. 27–35; Brian Woodcock, *Medieval Ecclesiastical Courts in the Diocese of Canterbury,* generally; Richard Wunderli, *London Church Courts and Society on the Eve of the Reformation,* introduction; Norma Adams and Charles Donahue, Jr., eds., *Select Cases from the Ecclesiastical Courts of the Province of Canterbury c.1200–1301,* introductory essay. Wunderli and others note that the highest episcopal court, the bishop's consistory court, dealt primarily with civil instance cases, while the commissary court took cognizance of criminal and probate cases.

31. *Registrum Simonis de Gandavo, Diocesis Saresbirensis 1297–1315,* vol. 1, pp. 10–13 [Canterbury and York Series, vol. 40].

32. Ibid., pp. 12–13 ". . . Nos igitur tam penali iuri quod, licet vos latere nullatenus estimemus, ex habundanti cum presentibus inseri fecimus prout tenemur immo ut cogimur obedire volentes, vobis omnimoda qua circa premissa fungimur auctoritate firmiter iniungendo mandamus ne aliter quam ut ex forma dicte decretalis habetur egrediendo seu ad vos personas alienas ingredi promittendo vel sorores recipiendo quicquam ex nunc aliqualiter faciatur. Et licet hucusque non sinetibus impedimentis huiusmodi materialis vobis murorum ambitus nondum fiat tam legis prescripte quam religionis virtute voluntarie ut

1303, Simon of Ghent reissued his mandate, leaving out only the text of *Periculoso,* and sent it to the nuns of Wilton, Amesbury, Lacock, Tarrant Keynes and Kington.[33]

Another early effort was made by Robert Winchelsey, archbishop of Canterbury 1293–1313. A register entry dated May 23, 1299, enjoins the abbess and nuns of the Benedictine house of Malling to observe the prescriptions of the recent constitution of Boniface VIII about remaining enclosed and not accepting more nuns than the community is able to support.[34] Interestingly, although Winchelsey's lengthy injunction included allusions to and quotations from provincial legislation such as that of Ottobuono and Peckham, the archbishop gave *Periculoso* primacy of place. Judging from the wording, he wished to accord it recognition as a universal and hence supremely authoritative mandate.[35] Later the same year, Winchelsey sent a similar mandate to

---

de eo quod est necessarium virtus fiat secundum formam pretactam clause totaliter maneatis, vos et ea que ad clausuram huiusmodi necessaria dinoscuntur efficaciter disponentes ac eciam preparantes citra apud Ieiunii proxime jam futuri ut clausure predicte ordinacionem sacro inchohante Ieiunio Deo propicio valeamus salubriter inchoare et effaciter adimplere. Sin vero impedimentum racionale subsit quare fieri sic non possit, illud et quid feceritis et intenditis in premissis et ea tangentibus per patentes vestras litteras harum seriem sive cum tenore prescripte decretalis habentes infra octo dies post festum Purificacionis B. Virginis nobis apertius intimentur . . . Celestis sponsus in amorem sui vestra desideria exitet et incendat ut terrena sic vestris mentibus amarescant quod iucundum sit vobis ab omni mundane voluptatis occasione secludi."

33. Ibid., p. 109–10; These houses followed different rules: Wilton, Amesbury, and Kington were Benedictine monasteries, Lacock was an Augustinian house, and Tarrant Keynes was a Cistercian monastery: see Eileen Power, *Medieval English Nunneries,* Appendix IV, pp. 685–92.

34. *Registrum Roberti Winchelsey Cantuariensis Archiepiscopi 1294–1313,* vol. 2, pp. 833–37. His injunction begins: "In primis statuentes quod secundum consitucionem sanctissimi patris domini Bonifacii divina providencia sacrosancte Romane ac universalis ecclesie summi pontificis super religiosarum mulierum non mendicancium in suis monasteriis inclusione perpetua nuper editam, nulla decetero inter vos recipiantur aliqualiter in sororem donec numerus monialium vestri conventus decrescendo in tantum minuatur quod superexistentes incluse de bonis et proventibus ipsius monasterii congrue possint absque penuria sustentari"; p. 833.

35. See above; provincial legislation incorporated into the injunction subsequently includes paraphrases of Ottobuono's restrictions on "singularity" in dining, p. 835, and Peckham's restrictions on lengthy, nonessential conversations with outsiders, p. 834.

the Benedictine nuns of Sheppey—this injunction included the full text of *Periculoso*.[36]

In addition to spreading the news of papal cloister regulations to the nuns in his care, Archbishop Winchelsey also appears to have taken seriously Boniface VIII's directives regarding the elimination of occasions for "wandering." In 1300, he admonished the preceptor of the Hospitallers of Sutton at Hone to stop summoning the prioress of Davington to appear in person in his manorial court. From now on, he cautioned, given the stipulations of Boniface VIII, the preceptor must allow the prioress to conduct her business through a proctor or an attorney.[37] Winchelsey's actions paralleled those of Godfrey Giffard, bishop of Worcester. His notice, issued in 1300, set down exact diocesan guidelines: "As to the shutting up of nuns, it is expedient that a letter of warning be sent according to the form of the consititution *[Periculoso]* and directed to every house of nuns, that they do what is necessary for their inclusion . . ."[38]

Even greater zeal in the service of papal authority was shown by Bishop Dalderby of Lincoln. In 1300, having issued a directive to the archdeacons of his diocese empowering them to conduct preliminary visitations of the nuns under his jurisdiction, Dalderby himself visited the major houses in his diocese. At each one he explained *Periculoso* to the nuns (in the vernacular), commanded them to obey it, and left a copy of the decree with them. His directives were not, however, always warmly or even civilly received. An entry in Dalderby's register describes his reception at the Benedictine monastery of Markyate:

> On July 3rd, in the first year [of his consecration], the bishop visited the house of nuns of Markyate and on the following day he caused to be recited before the nuns of the same [house] in chapter the statute put forth by the lord Pope Boniface VIII concerning the enclosure of

36. Ibid., pp. 846–48.
37. Ibid., vol. 1, p. 389 "Ne igitur dicta priorissa ob hoc causam seu occasionem habeat devagrandi, vos monemus et hortamur in domino Iesu Christo quatinus procuratorem seu attornatum dicte priorisse ad faciendum huiusmodi sectam curie pro eadem admittatis, districciones factas pro personali secta huiusmodi penitus relaxantes et a similibus imposterum abstinentes sub pena canonice districcionis."
38. Quoted in Power, *Medieval English Nunneries*, p. 350.

nuns, explained it in the vulgar tongue and giving them a copy of the same statute under his seal, ordered them in virtue of obedience henceforth to observe it in the matter of enclosure and of all things contained in it and especially to close all doors by which entrance is had into the inner places of their house and to permit no person whether dishonest or honest, to enter in to them, without reasonable and manifest cause and licence from the person to whom [the granting of such a licence] pertains . . . But when the bishop was going away, certain of the nuns, disobedient to these injunctions, hurled the said statute at his back and over his head and as well the prioress as the convent appeared to consent to those who threw it, following the bishop to the outer gate of the house and declaring unanimously that they were not content in any way to observe such a statute.[39]

The active hostility of the nuns of Markyate did not deter Bishop Dalderby—he continued to send warning letters and to impose sentences of excommunication on recalcitrants. Other prelates were made of lesser stuff.[40] Throughout the fourteenth century, English bishops continued to issue injunctions about enclosure, many directly reproducing the wording of *Periculoso*.[41] They continued to do so even though their words (to judge from the number of times they had to be repeated) proved ineffectual.[42] They also, however, increasingly countenanced a less than rigorous application of that constitution.

In 1319, only twenty years after the promulgation of *Periculoso*, the set of rules that Walter Stapeldon, bishop of Exeter, addressed to the nuns of Polsloe (Benedictine) and Canonsleigh (Augustinian) were a far from exacting application of Boniface VIII's constitution. Permission of the superior and "reasonable cause" were required if a nun wished to leave her monastery, but such permission might be given

39. Ibid., pp. 351–52.
40. Ibid., p. 353.
41. Ibid.; Power mentions the 1329 mandate of Bishop Grandisson of Exeter and that of his successor, Bishop Brantyngham in 1376; see also *The Registers of Roger Martival, Bishop of Salisbury 1315–1330*. In 1322 he appointed a delegate to visit nunneries as required by "a new papal constitution" (vol. 2 p. 382), and he sent several notices to the nuns of Shaftesbury limiting new admissions in view of their limited revenues (vol. 2 pp. 409–10 and 574–78).
42. Ibid., p. 416; orders demanding the removal of seculars at Godstow, for example, were reiterated by successive ordinaries.

once a year. A nun who went to visit friends at some distance was expected to return *within a month*, but even this generous stay might be lengthened "in the case of death, or of the known illness of herself or of her near friends."[43] In 1329 Stapeldon's successor, John Grandisson, shortened the length of a permitted absence to fifteen days—still something less than the Bonifacian ideal—and a maximum of three weeks became a common time limit by the mid-fourteenth century in a variety of dioceses.[44]

The willingness of at least some English bishops to compromise the high ideals embodied in *Periculoso* is also evident in the extent to which they granted special licenses abrogating particular elements of claustration. *Periculoso* had implied that such exemptions should be granted only for compelling reason *(rationabilis et manifesta causa)* and sparingly. English ordinaries of the fourteenth and fifteenth centuries seem to have proffered them readily. In 1391, while forbidding the nuns of Canonsleigh to shelter seculars in their monasteries, Bishop Brantyngham of Exeter excepted two nobles, a man and a woman, already residing there; similar exemptions were granted to widows, the elderly, and small children.[45] In 1314 Archbishop Greenfield granted a special license to a nun of Yedingham to visit relatives to recover her health; in 1368, the abbess of Shaftesbury received a license to live on her manors for a year in order to take the air.[46]

By far the greatest number of licenses were granted by bishops to wealthy and important secular women seeking temporary residence in a nunnery. In 1305, Bishop William Greenfield of York granted a license to the niece of Sir John de Burton, under five years of age, to be received by the convent of Appelton; four years later, he wrote to the same convent, licensing them to receive the young niece of Sir William de Jafford for the space of four years.[47] In 1310 the bishop granted permission to Agnes de Frythefy, a laywoman, to live as a per-

---

43. Ibid., p. 355; Power quotes in full from the registers of William Stapeldon.

44. Ibid., pp. 356–57.   45. Ibid., pp. 416–17.

46. Ibid., p. 362.

47. *The Register of Archbishop Greenfield (1306–1315)*, vol. 152, p. 97; vol. 149, p. 70.

manent resident at the convent of Sinningthwaite, and in 1315, he granted a license to the prioress of Hampole to sell a corrody (the right to room and board) to Joan, daughter of Sir Richard Vernon.[48] Bishop Ralph of Shrewsbury granted two laywomen a special license for a four-month stay at the monastery of Cannington in 1336, and in 1354 allowed Isolda, wife of John Bycombe, to reside in the same monastery for nearly half a year.[49]

It should be noted here that while English bishops consistently licensed the entrance of seculars to "cloistered" convents, the papacy only made the list of those so privileged even longer. Throughout the fourteenth and fifteenth centuries, popes regularly granted permission to great ladies, and their frequently large entourages, to enter "cloistered" English convents. In 1391, for example, Boniface IX granted Anne, Queen of England, permission to enter enclosed women's communities "with fifty honest persons any time she pleased"—albeit not to spend the night; in the same year he licensed the duke and duchess of Gloucester to enter those houses "six times a year with twenty persons."[50]

By the fifteenth century, papal licenses to important English seculars tended to become even more general and to accommodate overnight stays as well. In 1408, for instance, Pope Gregory XII granted Philippa, duchess of York, the right to enter monasteries "of enclosed nuns of any orders in England," with five or six honest matrons or virgins as often as she pleased, and to stay for as long as three days and nights at a time.[51] In 1411, the same pope allowed Lucy, countess of Kent, to enter any enclosed English community with six honest ladies, "to eat and to pass the night therein at her own expense."[52]

With some casuistry, virtually every "special license" granted by a pope or local ordinary could be subsumed under *Periculoso*'s saving clause. The *rationabilis et manifesta causa* given by Boniface VIII as the

---

48. Ibid., vol. 2, pp. 84–85, 220.

49. Power, *Medieval English Nunneries*, p. 410.

50. *Calendar of Entries in the Papal Registers Relating to Great Britain and Ireland*, vol. 4 (1362–1404), pp. 397, 394.

51. Ibid., vol. 6 (1404–15), p. 132.

52. Ibid., vol. 6, p. 293; see also Power, *Medieval English Nunneries*, p. 418, for many more examples of papal licenses granted to prominent people.

rationale for granting special licenses could be, and was, used as grounds to approve the many and various trips, excursions, and transfers made by ostensibly cloistered nuns, as well as the entrance of seculars into their midst. Perhaps most at odds with the spirit as well as the letter of *Periculoso* were the exemptions granted by English bishops to those secular persons of all ages who actually wished to board with enclosed nuns.

As Eileen Power's thorough documentation of convent-sponsored education (1250–1537) illustrates, children of both sexes continued to be a part of female monastic life, long after the promulgation of *Periculoso*.[53] Ironically, most of our information on these children comes from episcopal prohibitions (usually based upon a recent visitation) against disruptive adult boarders. Thus, in 1359 Bishop Gynewell of Lincoln prohibited all boarders at Elstow, *except* for girls under ten and boys under six.[54] In the fifteenth century, successive bishops in the same diocese continued their general prohibitions, while at the same time raising the allowable age for schoolchildren—fourteen for girls and ten for boys.[55] In 1309, Archbishop Greenfield of York ordered his official to remove all secular women *over the age of twelve* from nunneries in his diocese, and in 1310 he directed the prioress of St. Clement's York to do the same—with an additional exception this time, of "washerwomen and the servants of Thomas Leake's daughter."[56] By the fifteenth century, episcopal injunctions against boarders, whether schoolchildren or adults, focus more often on keeping seculars from certain areas of a convent, or on keeping certain types of boarders out, rather than on excluding seculars altogether. Bishop Alnwick's vist to Harrold in 1442–43, for example, resulted in a prohibition of secular persons, whether women or children, from lying in the nuns' dormitory at night.[57] At Hampole in 1411, the prioress was ordered not

53. See Power, *Medieval English Nunneries,* Note B, pp. 568–75 for printed references to convent education in England 1250–1537.
54. Ibid., pp. 262–63.
55. Ibid.
56. *Register of Archbishop Greenfield 1306–1315,* vol. 1, p. 127; vol. 2, pp. 80–81; It will be recalled that this same archbishop granted special licenses for two adult corrodians (see note 19 above).
57. Power, *Medieval English Nunneries,* p. 569 and pp. 408–9, regarding secular women in dormitories.

to allow any corrodiary to keep "suspected women" with her in the house.[58] And in 1432 at the monastery of Godstow, Bishop Gray ordered "that Felmersham's wife with her whole household, and other women of mature age be utterly removed from the monastery within one year next to come, seeing that they are a cause of disturbance to the nuns and an occasion of bad example by reason of their attire and those who come to visit them."[59]

William Lyndwood's censure of English ordinaries gains credibility when we observe the way in which, in the wake of *Periculoso,* episcopal injunctions grew more flexible and "special licenses" more ubiquitous. Whether this happened in response to pressure exerted by prominent individuals or to the resistence of the nuns themselves, the much-needed revenues that short- and long-term pensioners brought in, and the economic interests served by an abbess who went abroad on convent business, were factors in perpetuating the laxness. Schoolchildren boarding with the nuns or the temporary absence of an abbess on business were indeed technical breaches of strict enclosure, but bending the rules of *Periculoso* continued to appear to be vital to the economic welfare of nuns. As late as the pre-dissolution visits of 1535 this view was articulated by ordinaries as well as abbesses.[60] Apostasy, on the other hand, the full-blown and apparently permanent rejection of one's religious profession, as well as one's monastic cloister, was a different matter.

At the close of *Periculoso,* Boniface VIII had stated that ordinaries

58. Ibid., p. 414.
59. Ibid., pp. 413–14.
60. The set of injunctions that Cromwell's visitors carried with them included a severely worded article on strict enclosure of all monks and nuns, including superiors. Enforcing the injunction would have led to inevitable disobedience, punishable by suppression. See David Knowles, *Bare Ruined Choirs,* pp. 160–68. Even one of the visitors, Ap Rice, objected to such strict enclosure stating that "for as many of these houses stand by husbandry they must fall to decay if the heads are not allowed to go out" (Power, *Medieval English Nunneries,* p. 72 note 1). Power also quotes the eloquent letter of the last abbess of Wilton to Cromwell, defending her need to oversee personally the business of "this poor house which is in great debt and requireth much reparation and also which without good husbandry is not like, in long season, to come forward . . ." p. 72.

who remained uncooperative in their duty to enclose nuns under their jurisdiction were "to be constrained through ecclesiastical censure, with no right of appeal, invoking for this, if necessary, the aid of the secular arm."[61] In England, civil authority came to be exerted directly on defiant monks or nuns. Presupposing a well-intentioned ordinary but a recalcitrant nun, the writ *de apostata capiendo* uniquely reflected the pope's wished-for cooperation between sacred and secular powers. Parallel in many ways to the writ for the the the capture of excommunicates, *de apostata capiendo* would be issued by the crown upon receipt of a petition for the return of an apostate nun—that is, a professed religious who had left the convent without permission and who intended not to return.[62] The petition itself would normally come from the head of the religious house or, occasionally, from the bishop of the diocese.[63] In 1382 the prioress of the Benedictine monastery of Haliwell received a writ *de apostata capiendo* for the return of the nun Elizabeth Arundell. The king sent a four-man commission, including a sergeant-at-arms and a chaplain, to apprehend the apostate.[64] A similar commission was empaneled in 1405 to search for and return a nun of Rowney (also Benedictine); chancery records as well as episcopal registers attest to a reliance on this method of enforcement of monastic

61. ". . . invocato ad hoc, si opus fuerit, auxilio brachii saecularis." See the Appendix for the full text of *Periculoso*.

62. I am concerned here with nuns, but this writ was issued even more often for the return of wayward monks, as the recent research of F. Donald Logan indicates: "Runaway Religious: Problems of Relgious Apostacy in Medieval England," unpublished paper delivered before the New England Historical Association meeting, April 20, 1991; I have referred to this paper frequently for details concerning the documentary evidence as well as the procedural forms. For his paper, Professor Logan used PRO Chancery 81, "Warrants for the Great Seal" exclusively—an admittedly incomplete source containing 354 petitions for the writ *de apostato capiendo* naming 467 apostates, only 9 of whom were women. For a much fuller discussion of this issue, see Logan's recently published monograph, *Runaway Religious in England, c. 1240–1540*. Eileen Power (see below) looked at chancery warrants as well as some episcopal registers in which she found a good sampling of female apostates.

63. Power, *Medieval English Nunneries*, p. 442 note 2.

64. Ibid., p. 442; Unfortunately, as Logan has pointed out, the ultimate disposition of most of these cases is unknown; so too, the motives of most apostates.

discipline well into the sixteenth century.[65] When and if the apostate was returned, or returned of her own will, she would seek absolution from the bishop of her diocese. At his behest the convent would be compelled to readmit her, imposing strict discipline upon her.[66]

In sum, although *Periculoso* was accepted early, and some might even say eagerly, by the English episcopacy, its enforcement remained a difficult if not impossible matter. Faced with opposition from the nuns themselves, as well as from their secular patrons and beneficiaries, local ordinaries seem to have been willing to temper the strict regulations of *Periculoso*. In part, they did so by superimposing existing provincial legislation upon the decree. While careful to direct the comings and goings of nuns, the injunctions of Stephen Langton and John Peckham had generally appreciated that some latitude on the subject of enclosure was not incompatible with well-ordered female monasticism. When nuns attempted serious breach of enclosure rules, however —when, in Boniface VIII's words, "casting off the reins of respectability and impudently abandoning nunnish modesty [they] wander[ed] about outside of their monasteries"—the English church showed itself uniquely responsive. English ordinaries and monastic superiors were, at least in this respect, well equipped to enforce monastic discipline by enlisting the aid of the crown itself—a measure whose effectiveness can only be gauged by the fact that writs *de apostata capiendo* continued to be sued out of chancery for three centuries.

65. Ibid., p. 443; p. 442 note 2 lists several fourteenth-century petitions; pp. 456–57 cites incidents from episcopal registers.

66. See the mandate of Archbishop Greenfield to the nuns of Appelton ordering them to re-admit Agnes of York who "ad nos in humilitatis spiritu redeuntem, a sentencia excommunicacionis majoris quam pro temeraria habitus sui mutacione et apostasia de vestro monasterio absque licencia recedendo et in seculo diucius evagando dampnabiliter incurrebat, absolvimus . . ." *Register of Archbishop Greenfield 1306–1315* vol. 2 p. 219.

Conclusion

In July 1616 Francis de Sales wrote to Cardinal Robert Bellarmine seeking advice about his newly formed Congregation of the Visitation. Heretofore unenclosed, the Visitation lacked the status of an approved religious order, and Francis wished to reconcile his desire that his nuns have an active apostolate with his conviction that only the title of religious order would ultimately preserve the Congregation. The cardinal responded with a surprising counsel, supported by a capsule history of the evolution of the canon law of the cloister:

> I would therefore retain the virgins and widows in their present state [without cloister or solemn vows], and not change something that is good. Prior to the time of Boniface VIII there were nuns in the Church both in the East and in the West. The Latin fathers, Cyprian, Ambrose, Jerome, and Augustine, and also the Greek fathers, Athanasius, Basil, Chrysostom, and others mentioned them. These nuns were not enclosed in monasteries in such a way that they could not go out when there was work to be done. You should be aware, your Grace, that before God, simple vows are not less binding nor less meritorious than solemn vows. The solemnity, as the cloister itself, was begun as an ecclesiastical practice by the same Boniface VIII.[1]

1. Cain, "Cloister," p. 446, translation his. Note that Bellarmine credits

The words of Cardinal Bellarmine, expressed more than three centuries after the publication of *Periculoso,* point up both Boniface VIII's achievement and the inherent weakness of his constitution. While acknowledging that *Periculoso* revolutionized the canon law of enclosure for women, Bellarmine failed to find spiritual perfection solely in the style of life it prescribed. Prepared to abide by its norms, he viewed those norms as manmade, a part of the jurisdictional, not the evangelical church, and he consequently found no reason to accord special sanctity to religious women who bound themselves by its rules. He did not, in short, subscribe to the Bonifacian ideal of exclusive, "true" religious practice, and he was not alone.

Displaying a marked antipathy to unorthodox religious activity by women, especially wandering and preaching ones, Boniface VIII had striven for uniformity of observance and a clear distinction between nuns and all other quasi-religious groups. Long before Cardinal Bellarmine's time, however—indeed almost immediately after the publication of *Periculoso*—religious women, local ordinaries, and even subsequent popes found such distinctions constraining. The popularity of simple vows and the multiplication of third orders, two trends which the pre-Trent papacy did nothing to resist and in fact often fostered, testify to the irrepressible tendency to find alternatives to the contemplative and isolated life of the cloistered nun.[2]

Among the nuns themselves (those clearly bound by solemn profes-

---

Boniface VIII with making solemn vows an integral part of church practice. The distinction between simple and solemn vows, although amorphous, had been established by the twelfth century, see: A. Vermeersch, "Vows," in *The Catholic Encyclopedia,* ed. Charles Herbermann et al. (New York: Encyclopedia Press Inc., 1913). vol. 15, pp. 511–14. Bellarmine doubtless refers to Boniface VIII's specific reference to simple and solemn vows in the *Liber Sextus* 3.15.1, the rubric of which reads: "Votum solemnisatum per susceptionem sacri ordinis vel per professionem factam alicui de religionibus per sedem apostolicam approbatis, dirimit matrimonium post contractum; alias solum impedit, et non dirimit."

2. On the significance of tertiaries and penitents see: Cain, "Cloister," pp. 273–78; on the prevalence of simple vows see especially: Emil Jombart and Marcel Viller, "Clôture" *DS,* vol. II, p. 10003; Soeur Marie-Amélie Le Bourgeois,"Dieu aime-t-il les murs?" p. 23; Harline, "Actives and Contemplatives."

sion to a monastic rule and hence to obey *Periculoso*), enforcement of strict enclosure appears to have been a problem. As the English record suggests and sympathetic canonists such as John Acton and William Lyndwood testify, both the nuns and those whose job it was to enclose them often had divided if not overtly hostile feelings about the process. Nor was there uniformity in the work of the academic canonists who glossed *Periculoso*.

Beginning with Joannes Monachus, jurists raised the difficult question of whether *Periculoso* actually increased the harshness of existing monastic rules for nuns. If it did, to what extent (and by what authority) were nuns who had been professed under a less stringent rule obligated by its provisions? At issue was nothing less than the legislative supremacy of papal mandates. While most canonists adroitly upheld that supremacy—by claiming with Joannes Monachus that enclosure rules really added nothing onerously new to existing rules, or with Joannes Andreae that, by virtue of their vow of obedience, nuns (and monks, as opposed to secular clergy) automatically relinquished their right to object to restrictions placed upon them by lawful superiors—some were clearly not so inclined. Petrus de Ancarano openly expressed his view that nuns who were unwilling to abide by strict enclosure should not be forced to do so, favoring an additional probationary year in which novices might assess their ability to commit to such a life. Joannes Koelner de Vanckel carefully delineated special circumstances that might exempt nuns from following the letter of *Periculoso* and made a point of reminding his readers that legislation, even papal legislation, could not bind those living in a region in which it had not been received—reception of *Periculoso* being an evident problem especially in parts of France and in Venice.

Furthermore, there was a curious inconsistency, at least in the formative era, in the commentary on *Periculoso*—an apparent unwillingness to treat *Periculoso* as the innovation that it was. Although faced with a decree that demanded special restrictions on the activities of nuns, such canonists as Guido de Baysio supported it by adducing counsels about enclosure that had been directed to monks! Wedded to an ancient ecclesiastical tradition that advised both monks and nuns to seek release from the cares of the world and to remain permanently within the precincts of monastic enclosure, continental jurists regularly followed in Guido de Baysio's footsteps. Even as late as the fifteenth century, William Lyndwood used *Periculoso* to support a provincial statute that concerned both monks and nuns—demonstrating, as Lyndwood put it, that all rulings on religious enclosure contained similar directives.

Gradually, however, the ideal of monastic equality receded, while the elaboration of the juridical details related to the enclosure of nuns continued apace. Dutifully the canonists glossed, clarified, and added stipulations to *Periculoso*. Where Boniface VIII had been vague, the canonists were specific: license to enter a female monastery was to be provided not by the abbess but by the ordinary; the entourage of the abbess when she was required to travel was to consist of two elderly monks and her chaplain; not even monks were to enter the cloister without a license; speech with the nuns was to be kept to a minimum. Where *Periculoso* had been silent, the canonists spoke. They determined that the penalty for infraction of the decree was to be excommunication, specified the circumstances in which a nun might leave her monastery without a license, listed the professionals who might be allowed to enter the cloister (barbers, physicians, etc.), and decided that abbesses, unlike abbots, were not to conduct visitations of the houses under their supervision.

Regardless of their nationalities and irrespective of their individual tendencies to sympathize with the plight of nuns or local ordinaries, regardless of whether they were laymen or high-ranking members of the clergy, and irrespective of the doubts they sometimes expressed, the important jurists prior to Trent ultimately supported the dictates of *Periculoso*. They upheld the idea, implicit in the decree, that what might have been advisable for the spiritual development of both monks and nuns was absolutely crucial for nuns. They even went further, adding special provisions that applied exclusively to women. Given the conservative nature of the canonists, as seen in their reluctance to jettison the ideal of equality between monks and nuns, how did they justify these distinctions based solely on gender?

First, and most obviously, their arguments hinged on the legal fact that nuns could never be ordained. As Gratian, the twelfth-century "father of canon law," had so painstakingly illustrated in his tractate on monasticism, monasteries could be seedbeds for those whose probity of life recommended them for promotion to the priesthood.[3] Acknowledging the number of hallowed ancient authorities who warned against the unnecessary involvement of monks in worldly affairs, Gratian had nevertheless found legitimate moral ground for a monk's assumption of pastoral duties, namely, obedience to his abbot and the needs of his church. These needs, in turn, could and did lead monks as far up the ladder of ecclesiastical preferment as the papacy itself. Lacking any such legitimate reason for departure from their monasteries, as Petrus de Perusio had pointed out, nuns were especially suited to observing absolutely what for monks could only be a counsel to perfection.

Second, the canonists assumed that although sexual abstinence and virginity were central values, essential to any life of religious dedication, nuns were specially blessed (or burdened) with an obligation to preserve a chastity that took on almost mythical significance and importance. Guido de Baysio set the tone by choosing to gloss, and to differentiate between, the words *modestia* and *verecundia*. He defined the latter as active avoidance of all impurity and a dread of contamination. Joannes Ándreae stressed that continence as well as virginity were included in the term chastity, and he equated the holiness of nuns with that single virtue. Commentators on *Periculoso* consistently regarded the preservation of chastity as an activity that outweighed all others. There is scarcely a hint in the literature that women religious might encounter any other moral dangers, nor that the cultivation of other virtues might be in order. Producing a particularly restrictive concept of what the religious life ought to be about, this obsession with female sexual purity confirms the observations of Jane Schulenburg and others that the rationale for cloistering nuns had shifted substantially during the Late Middle Ages.[4] Adopted in the early church as a means to an end, as a way to provide dedicated women with a safe haven in turbulent times, enclosure grew steadily more central to the institutional church. In view of the canonical comment of the four-

3. Gratian, *Decretum*, C. 16 q. 1 in particular.
4. Schulenburg, "Strict Active Enclosure . . . ," p. 79.

teenth and fifteenth centuries, enclosure had already become an end in itself, to which other values of religious life were increasingly subordinated.

Following a well-worn if not recently trodden path and buttressed by contemporary arguments endorsing papal supremacy, Boniface VIII's decree was seen as a reasonable, if harsh, corrective to the "frailties" of women—"deficiencies" that were never questioned, since they too were so consistently evinced in both Roman law and Holy Scripture. Such uniformity of canonical opinion in turn created the bedrock upon which the Church would continue to build. To become a recognized religious order after 1298, communities of women would have to subscribe to strict enclosure. They did so consistently. All new orders founded between 1300 and 1500 built cloister restrictions into their rules.[5] Nor was *Periculoso*'s impact felt only by nuns. Women in third orders and those outside of established orders were increasingly subject to legislation that sought to bring their active apostolate more into line with that of their cloistered sisters. Pope Leo X's rule for Regular Franciscan Tertiaries, promulgated in 1521, for instance, allowed strict enclosure for those desiring it—a stipulation not contained in the 1289 rule for the Franciscan Third Order Secular.[6] Among the "quasi-religious," the Beguines were most notably affected by the thinking articulated in *Periculoso* and its commentary. As Walter Simons had convincingly argued, the great beguinages of the southern Low Countries did not arise spontaneously but were the result of conscious intervention by ecclesiastical and secular authorities. Thus, only the *curtis* type of beguinage, home of the *beguinae clausae*, survived the persecution of the fourteenth century.[7]

5. Jean Leclerq, "La Clôture," p. 572 mentions the new (or reformed) orders founded by St. Bridget of Sweden (1346), Blessed Angela of Foligno (1393), St. Colette (1410) and the first Carmelites (1453); see also: Peter Anson, "Papal Enclosure for Nuns," pp. 121–22.

6. Pope Leo X's rule for Regular Franciscan Tertiaries, promulgated in 1521, *Bullarium Romanum*, vol. 5, pp. 764–67; see Cain, note 2 above, for a good discussion of the trend toward cloistered tertiary communities.

7. Walter Simons, "The Beguine Movement," pp. 86–91. Florence Koorn, "Women without Vows" suggests that the Sisters of the Common Life, extra-regular followers of the *Devotio Moderna*, were subject to the same pressures.

Consistent canonical opinion was also the wellspring from which, more than 250 years after its promulgation, a renewed and reaffirmed *Periculoso* emerged. In its final session, the great reforming Council of Trent not only renewed Boniface VIII's decree (using many of the same terms) but added sanctions, in the form of excommunication, for violators:

> Renewing the constitution of Boniface VIII which begins *Periculoso*, the holy council commands all bishops, calling the divine justice to witness and under threat of eternal damnation, to ensure that the enclosure of nuns in all monasteries subject to them by ordinary authority, and in others by the authority of the apostolic see, should be diligently restored where it has been violated, and preserved most carefully where it has remained intact; they should coerce any who are disobedient and refractory by ecclesiastical censures and other penalties, setting aside any form of appeal, and calling in the help of the secular arm if need be.[8]

That *Periculoso* as Boniface VIII composed it, with its sweeping provisions and lack of external sanctions, was not successfully implemented throughout Europe is not surprising. That it was an ideal striven for by monastic and episcopal officials from the time of its promulgation, that it continued to figure prominently in the law of the Church, and that it became the template for Tridentine renewal were

---

Note should be taken, however, of the continued existence of the active as well as contemplative ideal among women religious; see again, Craig Harline, "Actives and Contemplatives."

8. The relevant chapter (5) in session 25 of the Council of Trent (1563) begins: "Bonifatii VIII constitutionem, quae incipit *Periculoso*, renovans, sancta synodus universis episcopis sub obtestatione divini iudicii et interminatione maledictionis aeternae praecipit, ut in omnibus monasteriis sibi subiectis ordinaria, in aliis vero sedis apostolicae auctoritate clausuram sanctimonialium, ubi violata fuerit, diligenter restitui, et, ubi inviolata est, conservari maxime procurent, inobedientes atque contradictores per censuras ecclesiasticas aliasque poenas, quacumque appellatione postposita, compescentes, invocatio etiam ad hoc, si opus fuerit, auxilio brachii saecularis." *Decrees of the Ecumenical Councils*, vol. 2, pp. 777–78. It will be recalled that the jurists who glossed *Periculoso*, sensing that enforcement would be difficult without specific sanctions, had long held that those sanctions were implict in the decree—interpreting the word *acrimoniam* as the sentence of excommunication that Trent finally leveled.

largely the result of the interest and support it received from the academic jurists, who chose time and again to comment on, question, and, in short, keep alive, its message.[9]

9. Note that Pope Pius V further tightened the discipline prescribed by *Periculoso* in his constitution *Circa pastorialis* (1566), and again in 1569; still further admonitions to observe its precepts were published by Gregory XIII in 1572. The subsequent impact of *Periculoso* remains an underexamined topic. Cain, as cited, deals with some aspects of it and Soeur Marie-Amélie Le Bourgeois, "Dieu aime-t-il les murs?" briefly analyzes the impact of enclosure rulings on the seventeenth-century teaching orders. Craig Harline offers a needed corrective to earlier studies that tended to underestimate both the continued appeal of the contemplative life and the resilience of the active apostolate for women after Trent.

Appendix I

Text of the *Liber Sextus* Bull of Promulgation, *Sacrosanctae Romanae*, Friedberg ed., 2:933–36

Bonifacius, episcopus servus servorum Dei, dilectis filiis doctoribus et scholaribus universis Bononiae commorantibus salutem et apostolicam benedictionem.

Sacrosanctae Romanae ecclesiae, quam imperscrutabilis divinae providentiae altitudo universis dispositione incommutabili praetulit ecclesiis et totius orbis praecipuum obtinere voluit magistratum, regimini praesidentes, curis sollicitamur continuis, et assidua meditatione urgemur, et iuxta creditae nobis dispensationis officium subditorum commodis, in quorum prosperitate utique prosperamur, iugi quantum nobis ex alto concessum fuerit, sollicitudinis studio intendamus. Amplectimur quippe voluntarios pro ipsorum quiete labores et noctes quandoque transimus insomnes, ut scandala removeamus ab ipsis, et, quas humana natura, novas semper deproperans edere formas, lites quotidie invenire conatur, nunc antiquorum declaratione, nunc vero novorum editione iurium, prout nobis est possibile, reprimamus. Sane, quum post volumen decretalium, a felicis recordationis Gregorio Papa IX praedecessore nostro tam provide quam utiliter compilatum, nonnullae ab eo et ab aliis Romanis Pontificibus successive super diversis dicerentur articulis editae decretales, de quarum aliquibus, an decretales existerent, earumque auctoribus dubitabatur sollicite in iudiciis et in scholis: nos, ad apicem summi pontificatus superna dispositione vocati, super hoc cum instantia requisiti a multis, ambiguitatem et incertitudinem huiusmodi, dispendium pluribus afferentem, omnino tollere, ac elucidare, quae de decretalibus ipsis teneri, quaeve deberent in posterum refutari, gratia suffragante divina pro utilitate publica desiderabiliter affectantes, per venerabiles fratres nostros Guilielmum archiepiscopum Ebrudunensem, et Berengarium episcopum Biterensem, ac dilectum filium magistrum Richardum de Senis, sanctae Romanae ecclesiae vicecancellarium, iuris utriusque doctorem, decretales huiusmodi diligentius fecimus recenseri, et tandem, pluribus ex ipsis, quum vel temporales, aut sibi ipsis vel aliis iuribus contrariae, seu omnino superfluae viderentur, penitus resecatis reliquas quibusdam ex eis abbreviatis, et aliquibus in toto vel in parte mutatis, multisque correctionibus, detractionibus et additionibus, prout expedire vidimus, factis in ipsis, in unum librum cum nonnullis nostris constitutionibus, in quibus ad correctionem morum subditorumque quietem multa statuuntur salubria, fructus uberes Deo propitio in domo Domini allatura, et plurima in iudiciis et extra frequentata dubia deciduntur, redigi mandavimus, et sub debitis titulis collocari. Quem librum, quinque libris aliis dicti voluminis decretalium adnectendum, sextum censuimus nuncupari, ut idem volumen senarium, qui numerus est perfectus, librorum illo adiuncto numerum comprehendens, perfectam in rebus agendis formam tribuat et in moribus disciplinam. Nec sine causa morem praedecessorum nostrorum, qui,quum constitutiones aliquas promulgabant noviter, eas mandabant sub antiquarum serie situari, omisimus in hac parte servare. Haec enim fecimus, ne infinitos libros destrui, et alios non sine maximis dispendiis, laboribus et expensis de novo fieri oporteret. Universitati vestrae igitur per apostolica scripta mandamus, quaetenus librum huiusmodi cum multa maturitate digestum, quem sub bulla nostra vobis transmittimus, prompto suscipientes affectu, eo utamini de cetero in iudiciis et in scholis, nullas alias praeter illas, quae inseruntur aut specialiter reservantur in eo, decretales aut constitutiones, a quibuscunque nostris praedecessoribus Romanis Pontificibus post editionem dicti voluminis promulgatas, recepturi ulterius aut pro decretalibus habituri.

Translation of *Sacrosanctae Romanae*

Boniface, bishop, servant of the servants of God, to all of his beloved sons, doctors, and scholars residing at Bologna, salutation and apostolic benediction.

Presiding over the government of the holy Roman church which the inscrutable height of divine providence, by immutable arrangement, preferred to all churches and which it wished to obtain an extraordinary magisterium of the whole world, we are vexed with continual cares and urged on by assiduous meditation to attend to the interests of our subjects—in whose prosperity we surely prosper—according to the office of stewardship entrusted to us, with an eternal zeal of solicitude, to the extent that it has been granted to us from on high.

Indeed, we quietly embrace on their behalf, voluntary labors and nights spent in sleeplessness, so that we may remove scandal from them; we now suppress, insofar as is possible for us, by the declaration of ancient and the promulgation of new laws, the quarrels, which human nature, always hurrying to produce new things, tries daily to invent.

Subsequent to the publication of the volume of decretals compiled as circumspectly as usefully by our predecessor Pope Gregory IX, of happy memory, some decretals were said to have been issued by him and by other Roman pontiffs on diverse subjects and it was carefully questioned in the courts and in the schools whether these decretals existed and who their authors were. We, called to the highest summit of the priesthood by heavenly arrangement, being asked urgently by many on this account to remove completely such ambiguity and uncertainty that occasions a loss for so many, and to explain which of the decretals ought to be kept and which ought to be disregarded in the future, cause such decretals to be diligently examined by our venerable brothers William archbishop of Embrun, and Berengar bishop of Béziers and the beloved son master Richard of Siena vice-chancellor of the holy Roman church and doctor of both laws, and, at length, to be completely purged of those that contradict the times, themselves, or other laws or that seem entirely superfluous. The remainder, being abbreviated or changed in whole or in part by many corrections, deletions, and additions to the extent that it seems expedient, we directed to be collected into one book and placed under suitable titles together with some of our constitutions in which many salutary decisions are made for the correction of conduct and the peace of our subjects. (These will bear abundant fruit in the house of the Lord, God being gracious.) and in which very many frequent unsettled matters, inside and out of court, are decided.

We have decided to join this book to the preceding five and to name it *Sextus* so that that volume six, which is the perfect number, comprising the number of books when it is joined to them, may give perfect form in procedures and perfect discipline in practice.

Not without reason did we omit to preserve in this part the practice of our precedessors who, whenever they promulgated anew any constitutions, directed that they be listed under the sequence of the ancient ones. This indeed we did in order that countless books not be destroyed and others made anew at great labor and expense.

We therefore decree to all of you, through apostolic writings, that such a book, arranged with much care, which under our bull we transmit to you, be taken up with manifest affection, and be used henceforth in the courts and schools, and that after the publication of the aforesaid volume, no decretals or constitutions promulgated by our Roman papal predecessors outside of those especially inserted in and reserved to the aforesaid volume be received or held as decretals.

Text of *Liber Sextus* 3.16 De statu regularium c. un. "Periculoso" Friedberg ed., 2:1053–54; collated with Vatican Borghese 7 *Liber Sextus* fol. 56v–57v.

Periculoso et detestabili quarundam monialium statui, (quae, honestatis laxatis habenis et monachali modestia sexusque verecundia impudenter abiectis, extra sua monasteria[1] nonnunquam per habitacula saecularium personarum discurrunt, et frequenter infra eadem monasteria personas suspectas admittunt, in illius, cui suam integritatem voluntate spontanea devoverunt,

---

1. *nonnunquam . . . personarum* omitted in text but added in margin

gravamen, offensam, in[2] religionis opprobrium et scandalum plurimorum,) providere salubriter cupientes, praesenti constitutione perpetuo irrefragabiliter valitura sancimus, universas et singulas moniales, praesentes atque futuras, cuiuscunque religionis[3] sint vel[4] ordinis, in quibuslibet mundi partibus exsistentes, sub perpetua in suis monasteriis debere de cetero permanere clausura ita, quod nulli earum, religionem tacite vel[5] expresse professae, sit vel[6] esse valeat quacunque ratione vel[7] causa, (nisi forte tanto et tali morbo evidenter earum aliquam laborare constaret, quod non posset cum aliis absque gravi periculo seu scandalo commorari,) monasteria ipsa deinceps egrediendi facultas; nullique aliquatenus inhonestae personae nec etiam honestae (nisi rationabilis et manifesta causa existat, ac de illius, ad quem pertinuerit, speciali licentia,) ingressus vel accessus pateat ad easdem,[8] ut sic a publicis et mundanis conspectibus separatae omnino servire Deo valeant liberius, et, lasciviendi opportunitate sublata eidem corda sua et corpora in omni sanctimonia diligentius custodire. &1 Sane, ut hoc salutare statutum commodius valeat observari, districtius inhibemus, ne in monasteriis ordinum non Mendicantium aliquae recipiantur de cetero in sorores, nisi quot poterunt de ipsorum monasteriorum bonis sive proventibus absque penuria sustentari, si secus actum fuerit, irritum decernentes. &2 Verum quando abbatissa vel[9] priorissa cuiusvis monasterii pro feudo, quod monasterium ipsum[10] tenet ab aliquo principe seu domino temporali, sibi debebit homagium vel[11] fidelitatis sacramentum praestare, (nisi, quod per procuratorem illud praestet, possit efficere apud eum,) de monasterio cum honesta et decenti societate exire poterit eo casu licenter, homagio facto, quam primum commode poterit, seu fidelitatis praestito sacramento ad ipsum monasterium e vestigio reversura, sic, quod in fraudem residentiae sive morae claustralis nihil fiat onmino. &3 Porro, ne moniales causam seu occasionem habeant evagandi, principes saeculares ac alios dominos temporales rogamus, requirimus, et obsecramus per viscera misericordiae Jesu Christi, eisdem in remissionem peccaminum nihilominus suadentes, quod abbatissas ipsas et priorissas ac moniales quascunque, monasteriorum suorum curam, administrationem negotiave gerentes, quibuscunque nominibus censeantur, per procuratores in suis tribunalibus seu curiis litigare permittant, ne pro constituendis procuratoribus, qui[12] atornati in aliquibus partibus nuncupantur, seu aliis huiusmodi easdem oporteat evagari. Si qui vero contra praesumpserint, exhortationi huiusmodi rationabili atque sanctae obtemperare nolentes, quum[13] sit iuri contrarium, quod mulieres, praesertim religiosae, per se ipsas litigare cogantur, et[14] a via deviet honestatis et periculum animarum inducat, ad hoc per suos ordinarios ecclesiasticos censura ecclesiastica compellantur. Episcopis autem et aliis praelatis superioribus et inferioribus quibuscunque iniungimus,

---

2. *in* omitted
3. *sint religione*
4. *vel > ut*
5. *vel > ut*
6. *vel > ut*
7. *vel > ut*
8. *, > . Ut . . .*
9. *vel > ut*
10. omit *ipsum*
11. *vel > ut*
12. *qui* omitted in text but added in margin
13. *quum > cui*
14. *et* omitted

quod et ipsi causas seu negotia, quae praefatae moniales habebunt agere coram ipsis aut in curiis eorundem, sive sint homagia, fidelitatis sacramenta, lites vel quicquid aliud, ipsa per procuratores earum fieri faciant et tractari. &4 Et quoniam parum esset condere iura, nisi essent qui ea exsecutioni debitae demandarent: patriarchis, primatibus, archiepiscopis et episcopis universis districte in virtute sanctae obedientiae sub obtestatione divini iudicii et interminatione maledictionis aeternae praecipiendo mandamus, quatenus eorum quilibet in civitate ac dioecesi propria in monasteriis monialium sibi ordinario iure subiectis sua, in iis[15] vero que ad Romanam immediate spectant ecclesiam sedis apostolicae auctoritate abbates vero et alii tam exempti quam non exempti prelati ecclesiarum, monasteriorum , et ordinum quorumcunque in monasteriis huiusmodi[16] sibi subiectis, de clausura convenienti, ubi non est, ipsorum monasteriorum expensis et fidelium eleemosynis, quas ad hoc procurent, diligentius facienda, et de ipsis monialibus includendis quam primum commode poterunt providere procurent, si divinae ac nostrae indignationis voluerint acrimoniam evitare,[17] contradictores atque rebelles per censuram ecclesiasticam appellatione postposita compescendo,[18] invocato ad hoc, si opus fuerit, auxilio brachii saecularis. Per hoc autem in monasteriis exemptiis ordinarii locorum quoad alia nullam sibi credant iurisdictionem vel potestatem aliquatenus attributam.

Translation of *Periculoso*

Wishing to provide for the dangerous and abominable situation of certain nuns, who, casting off the reins of respectability and impudently abandoning nunnish modesty and the natural bashfulness of their sex, sometimes rove about outside of their monasteries to the homes of secular persons and frequently admit suspect persons into these same monasteries, to the injury of that to which by free choice they vowed their chastity, to the disgrace and dishonor of the religious life and the temptation of many, we do firmly decree by this present constitution which shall forever remain in force, that nuns collectively and individually, both at present and in future, of whatsoever community or order, in whatever part of the world they may be, ought henceforth to remain perpetually cloistered in their monasteries, so that none of them, tacitly or expressly professed, shall or may for whatever reason or cause (unless by chance any be found to be manifestly suffering from a disease of such a type and kind that it is not possible to remain with the others without grave danger or scandal), have permission hereafter to leave their monasteries; and that no persons, in any way disreputable, or even respectable, shall be allowed to enter or leave the same (unless a reasonable and obvious cause exists, for which the appropriate authority may grant a special license) so that [the nuns] be able to serve God more freely, wholly separated from the public and worldly gaze and, occasions for lasciviousness having been removed, may most diligently safeguard their hearts and bodies in complete chastity.

15. *iis* > *huius*
16. *huiusmodi* omitted in text but added in margin
17. , > . *Contradictores*   18. , > . *Invocato*

 1. Indeed, so that this salutary statute be more easily observed, we most strictly decree that no sisters shall from this time forward be received in monasteries other than [those of] mendicant orders unless those same monasteries are able to support them with goods or revenues and without penury; contrary actions shall be considered void.

 2. But when an abbess or prioress of any monastery shall need to present herself to do homage or swear feality for a fief that the same monastery holds from any prince or temporal lord (unless, she can do so by a procurator representing her in his presence) she may leave the monastery, in this instance licitly, with respectable and decent company; having done homage or sworn the oath of fealty, let her return to the monastery as soon as it is conveniently possible, so that nothing whatever be done that impairs residence or enclosure.

 3. Further, lest nuns have any cause or occasion to go abroad we ask, we beg, and we beseech secular princes and other temporal lords, through the merciful heart of Jesus Christ, exhorting them that for the remission of sins, they allow the same abbesses and prioresses or nuns who carry out the administration of business for their monasteries, by whatever titles they may be designated, to litigate in their tribunals and courts through procurators, who in some places are called attorneys, or others of this kind, lest for lack of procurators the nuns themselves be required to go abroad. If anyone presume otherwise and refuse to comply with this kind of reasonable and holy exhortation, since it is against the law to require women, especially religious women, to litigate for themselves, and departs from the honorable path, and may lead to the peril of souls, let them be compelled to do this by their ecclesiastical ordinaries through ecclesiastical censures. Indeed we enjoin bishops and other prelates, whether inferior or superior, that when the aforesaid nuns have to come before them or into their courts for lawsuits or business or to do homage or swear fealty, or for disputes or anything else, that they be allowed to take their actions and transact their business through procurators.

 4. And since it would be pointless indeed to make laws unless someone were designated to enforce them, we strictly enjoin patriarchs, primates, archbishops, and all bishops in virtue of holy obedience, under threat of divine judgement and the prospect of eternal damnation, that they take very diligent care that the nuns of any monasteries within their city or diocese subject to them by law as ordinaries and indeed even those that are immediately subject solely to the authority of the Roman church and apostolic see, also abbots and others, exempt as well as non- exempt prelates of the church, with monasteries of whatsoever order subject to them, diligently enforce enclosure in those monasteries in which it is not observed as soon as they can properly provide for this; they shall meet the expenses incurred therein from the alms that they shall procure from the faithful for this purpose if they wish to evade our wrath and divine indignation; those who refuse and resist ought to be constrained through ecclesiastical censure, with no right of appeal, invoking for this, if necessary, the aid of the secular arm. Ordinaries should be aware, however, that they do not acquire in virtue of this [letter] any jurisdiction or power in any other matter over monasteries that are otherwise exempt [from the ordinary's control].

Appendix II

Additional Commentators on the *Liber Sextus*

The following are commentators known to have written on the *Liber Sextus*, but their work either did not include *Periculoso* (as noted in the entry) or was unavailable for this study.

Antonio de Butrio, d.1408—*In Sextum Decretalium volumen Commentaria* (Venetiis: F. Zilettus, 1575); comments extend only as far as Book III, Title VII; see: Schulte, *QL* vol. 2 pp. 289–94; Smith, pp. 86–87; *DDC* vol. 1 pp. 630–31.

Benedictus Capra, d.1470—*Lectura in Sextum* no editions listed; see: Schulte, *QL* vol. 2 pp. 344–45.

Bernardus Raymundi, d.1311—*Apparatus* on the *Liber Sextus* MS Lat. 114, University of Pennsylvania Library, contains comments on Books I and II only; MS Bologna 217; see: *Traditio* 24 (1968): 505–6.

Guilelmus de Monte Lauduno, d.1343—*Lectura super sextum* (Toulouse, 1524); MS Angers 378; circulated principally in France and soon outdated by Joannes Andreae's *Glossa Ordinaria*; see: Schulte, *QL* vol. 2 pp. 197–99; Smith, p. 69; *DDC* vol. 5 pp. 1078–79.

Joannes ab Imola, d.1436—A commentary on the *Liber Sextus* is mentioned by contemporaries, but Schulte was unable to locate a copy; see: Schulte, *QL* vol. 2 pp. 296–98.

Joannes de Anania, d.1457—*Super Sexto Decretalium* (Milan, 1492); other editions at Lyon in 1546 and 1553; see: Schulte, *QL* vol. 2 pp. 320–22; Smith, p. 88; *DDC* vol. 6 pp. 88–89.

Niccolo de Tudeschi (Panormitanus), d.1445—*Lectura* (or) *Commentaria in Sextum* . While Schulte (*QL* vol. 2 pp. 312–13) mentions editions at Venice in

1479 and 1595, I have been unable to find Panormitanus's work on the *Sext* in printed form. It is not even included in the *Omnia quae extant commentaria* (Venice, 1588). I have not located a manuscript of the *Lectura* in the United States.

Paulus Florentinus (Paolo Attavanti), d.1499—*Breviarium super tomum corpus iuris canonici* (Memingen: Albert Kume, 1499); see: Schulte, *QL* vol. 2 p. 401.

Petrus Bertrandus, d.1349—*Lectura in Sextum* text apparently no longer exists; see: Schulte, *QL* vol. 2 pp. 235–36; *DDC* vol. 2 pp. 789–91.

Philippus Franchus de Franchis, d.1471—*In sextum decretalium librum commentarii* (Basileae: S. Henriceptri, 1581); *Lectura super Sexto* editions at Venice, 1499 and 1504; see: Schulte, *QL* vol.2 pp. 342–43.

Zenzelinus de Cassanis, d.1350—*Lectura super VI Decretalium* MSS Tours 596, Chartres 461, Berlin 166, St. Omer 440 (without text), Paris 16902; see: Schulte, *QL* vol. 2 pp. 199–200.

Bibliography

Reference Works

Boyle, Leonard E., O.P. *A Survey of the Vatican Archives and of Its Medieval Holdings*. Toronto: Pontifical Institute, 1972.

Fournier, Paul, and Gabriel Le Bras. *Histoire des collections canoniques en occident depuis les fausses décrétales jusqu'au décret de Gratien*. 2 vols. Paris, 1931–32.

Handbuch der Quellen und Literatur der neueren europäischen Privatrechtsgeschichte. Edited by Helmut Coing. 3 vols. in 5. Munich: C. H. Beck, 1973.

Kuttner, Stephan. *Repertorium der Kanonistik (1140–1234)*. Studi e Testi 71. Città del Vaticano, 1937.

Regesta Pontificum Romanorum. Edited by August Potthast. Vol. 2. Berlin: Rudolf de Decker, 1874–79.

Smith, J. A. Clarence. *Medieval Law Teachers and Writers*. Ottawa: University of Ottawa Press, 1975.

Stickler, Alfons M. *Historia iuris canonici Latini*. Turin: Pontificium Athenaeum Salesianum, 1950.

Van Hove, A. *Prolegomena*. 2d ed. Malines-Rome: Dessain, 1945.

von Schulte,J. Friedrich. *Die Geschichte der Quellen und Literatur des canonischen Rechts von Gratian bis auf die Gegenwart*. 3 vols. Stuttgart: F. Enke, 1875–77; reprint Graz: Akademische Druck- u. Verlagsanstalt, 1956.

Miscellaneous Primary Sources

Bernard, St. *Opera*. Edited by J. Leclercq, C. H. Talbot, H. M. Rochais, et al. 8 vols. in 9. Rome, 1957–77.

———. *On Consideration*. Translated by J. Anderson and E. Kennan. Kalamazoo, Michigan: Cistercian Publications, 1976.

Boniface VIII. *Liber Sextus*. In *Corpus iuris canonici*, edited by Emil Friedberg. Vol. 2. Leipzig: B. Tauchnitz, 1879; reprinted Graz: Akademische Druck- u. Verlagsanstalt, 1959.

———. Text of *Periculoso* collated with MS Vat. Borghese 7, *Liber Sextus* fol. 56v–57v.

———. *Les registres de Boniface VIII*. Edited by Georges Digard. Bibliothèque des écoles françaises d' Athenes et de Rome. Vol. 4. Paris, 1884.

Bullarium Romanum. 25 vols. Turin, 1857–72.

Calendar of Entries in the Papal Registers Relating to Great Britain and Ireland. Edited by W. H. Bliss, C. Johnson, and J. A. Twemlow. London, 1893–1960.

Corpus iuris civilis. Edited by Paul Krueger, Theodor Mommsen, Rudolf Schoell, and Wilhelm Kroll. 3 vols. Berlin: Weidmann, 1872–95.

Councils and Synods with Other Documents Relating to the English Church. Part II, 1265–1313, edited by M. Powicke and C. R. Cheney. Oxford: At the Clarendon Press, 1964.

Decrees of the Ecumenical Councils. Edited by Norman Tanner, S.J. 2 vols. Georgetown: Sheed and Ward, 1990.

Digest of Justinian. Latin text edited by Theodor Mommsen and Paul Krueger. English translation edited by Alan Watson. 4 vols. Philadelphia: University of Pennsylvania Press, 1985.

William Greenfield. *The Register of Archbishop Greenfield*. Edited by A. Hamilton Thompson. London: Bernard Quaritch, 1931–38; Surtees Society Publications, vols. 145, 149, 151–53.

The Letters of Abelard and Heloise. Edited and translated by Betty Radice. London: Penguin Books, 1974.

Roger Martival. *The Registers of Roger Martival, Bishop of Salisbury, 1315–1330*. Edited by Kathleen Edwards. Oxford: Oxford University Press, 1959–65.

Registrum Roberti Winchelsey, Cantuariensis archiepiscopi, A.D. 1294–1313. Edited by Rose Graham. Oxford: At the University Press, 1952–56.

Registrum Simonis de Gandavo Diocesis Saresbiriensis 1297–1315. Edited by C. T. Flower and M. C. Dawes. Oxford, 1934.

Sanctorum conciliorum nova et amplissima collectio. Edited by Giovanni Domenico Mansi. 31 vols. Florence–Venice 1759–98.

Statuta Captitulorum Generalium Ordinis Cisterciensis. Edited by D. J. M. Canivez. 8 vols. Louvain, 1933–41.

Tractatus universi iuris. 2d edition, 22 vols. in 28. Venice: Franciscus Zilettus, 1584–86.

Glosses

Dominicus de Santo Gemignano. *Super VI Decretalium*. Venetiis: Johannes de Colonia et Johannes Manthen, 1477.

Guido de Baysio. *Apparatus in Sextum*. Cambridge: Gonville and Caius College, MS 256/661.

Joannes Andreae. *Glossa Ordinaria ad Librum Sextum*. In *Corpus iuris canonici*. 4 vols. Venice: Apud Iuntas, 1605.

———. *Glossa Ordinaria*. In *Corpus iuris canonici*. 4 parts in 1 vol. Lugduni Apud Hugonem a Porta, et Antonium Vincentium, 1553.

———. *Liber Sextus decretalium cum Clementinis: sextus decretalium cum certis additionibus Johannus Andree*. Sebastianus Brant, 1500. Hain # 3626.

———. *Novella in Sextum*. Venetiis: Philippus Pincius, 1499; reprint Graz: Akademische Druck- u. Verlagsanstalt, 1963.

Joannes Monachus. *Glossa Aurea*. Paris: Jehan Petit, 1535; reprint Aalen: Scientia, 1968.

Johannes Koelner de Vanckel (Vanckel). *Summarium textuale et conclusiones super Sextum*, 1465. Hain # 9787.

Peter of Ancarano. *Lectura super Sexto decretalium*. Lyon: Johannes Moylin, 1535.

Treatises

Johannes Franciscus de Pavinis. *Tractatus visitationum*. In *Tractatus universi iuris*, vol. 14. Venice: Franciscus Zilettus, 1584–86.

John Acton. *Constitutiones legitime seu legatine regionis anglicane: cum subtilissima interpretatione doctorii Johannis de Athon*. Paris: J. Confluentinus, 1504.

Petrus de Perusio. *Tractatus status mutatione ecclesiarum*. In *Tractatus universi iuris*, vol. 14. Venice: Franciscus Zilettus, 1584–86.

Raymundus Fraguier. *Tractatus de relisiosis sectis eorumque auctoribus*. In *Tractatus universi iuris*, vol. 14. Venice: Franciscus Zilettus, 1584–86.

William Lyndwood. *Provinciale*. A. Brocard, 1501.

———. *Lyndwood's Provinciale*. Edited by J. V. Bullard and H. C. Bell. London: Faith Press, 1929.

Secondary Works

Anson, P. F. "Papal Enclosure for Nuns." *Cistercian Studies* 3 (1968) 109–23; 189–206.

Atkinson, Clarissa. "Precious Balsam in a Fragile Glass: The Ideology of Virginity in the Later Middle Ages." *Journal of Family History* (Summer 1983) 131–43.

Barraclough, Geoffrey. *The Medieval Papacy*. New York: Harcourt, Brace, and World, 1968.

Berman, Constance. "Women as Donors and Patrons to Southern French Monasteries in the Twelfth and Thirteenth Centuries." In *The Worlds of Medieval Women: Creativity, Influence, Imagination*, edited by Constance Berman, Charles Connell, and Judith Rothschild. Morgantown: West Virginia University Press, 1985.

Boase, T. S. R. *Boniface VIII*. London, 1933.

Bolton, Brenda. "Mulieres Sanctae." In *Women in Medieval Society*, edited by Susan Mosher Stuard. Philadelphia: University of Pennsylvania Press, 1976.

Boyd, Catherine. *A Cistercian Nunnery in Mediaeval Italy: The Story of Rifreddo in Saluzzo, 1220–1300*. Cambridge: Harvard University Press, 1943.

Boyle, Leonard E. "The Curriculum of the Faculty of Canon Law at Oxford in the First Half of the Fourteenth Century." In *Oxford Studies Presented to Daniel Callus*. Oxford: Oxford University Press, 1964.

Brooke, Rosalind and Christopher. "St. Clare." In *Studies in Church History, Subsidia I, Medieval Women*, edited by Derek Baker. Oxford: Basil Blackwell, 1978.

Brundage, James A. *Law, Sex, and Christian Society in Medieval Europe*. Chicago: University of Chicago Press, 1987.

———. *Medieval Canon Law*. London: Longman, 1995.

———. "The Cambridge Faculty of Canon Law and the Ecclesiastical Courts of Ely." In *Medieval Cambridge: Essays on the Pre-Reformation University*, edited by P. N. R. Zutshi. Woodbridge: Boydell, 1993.

Bruzelius, Caroline A. "Hearing Is Believing: Clarissan Architecture, ca. 1213–1340." *Gesta* 31/2 (1992): 83–91.

Bucher, Karl. *Die Frauenfrage im Mittelalter*. Tubingen: Laupp, 1910.

Bynum, Caroline Walker. *Jesus as Mother: Studies in the Spirituality of the High Middle Ages*. Berkeley: University of California Press, 1982.

———. *Holy Feast and Holy Fast: The Religious Significance of Food to Medieval Women*. Berkeley: University of California Press, 1987.

———. *Fragmentation and Redemption*. New York: Zone Books, 1991.

Cain, James R. "Cloister and the Apostolate of Religious Women." *Review for Religious* 27/2 (1968): 243–80, 27/4:652–71.

Cheney, C. R. "William Lyndwood's *Provinciale*." *The Jurist* 21, no. 4 (October 1961) 405–34.

———. "Legislation of the Medieval English Church." *English Historical Review* 50 (1935): 193–217.

Coing, Helmut. *Englishe und kontinentale Rechtsgeschichte: ein Forschungsprojekt*. Berlin: Duncker und Humblot, 1985.

Coleman, Janet. "Property and Poverty." In *The Cambridge History of Medieval Political Thought*, edited by J. H. Burns, pp. 607–48. Cambridge: Cambridge University Press, 1988.

Creusen, J. "Clôture." *Dictionnaire de droit canonique* 3:892–908. Paris, 1938.

Dolhagaray, B. "Clôture." *Dictionnaire de théologie catholique* 3:241–58. Paris, 1909–50.

Donahue, Charles. *Why the History of Canon Law Is Not Written*. London: Selden Society, 1986.

———, and Norma Adams. *Select Cases from the Ecclesiastical Courts of the Province of Canterbury c. 1200–1301*. London: Selden Society, 1981.

Duggan, Charles. *Twelfth-Century Decretal Collections and Their Importance in English History*. London, 1963.

Eckenstein, Lina. *Women under Monasticism*. New York: Russell and Russell, 1896.

Elvey, Elizabeth. *The Courts of the Archdeaconry of Buckingham, 1483–1523*. Aylesbury: Buckinghamshire Record Society, 1975.

de Fontette, Micheline. *Les religieuses à l'âge classique du droit canon: Recherches sur les structures juridiques des branches féminines des ordres*. Paris, 1967.

Freed, John B. "Urban Development and the 'Cura Monialium' in Thirteenth Century Germany." *Viator* 3 (1972): 311–27.

Garcia y Garcia, Antonio. "The Faculties of Law." In *A History of the University in Europe*. Vol. 1, edited by Hilde de Ridder Symoens. Cambridge: Cambridge University Press, 1992.

Gold, Penny. "The Charters of Le Ronceray d'Angers: Male/Female Interaction in Monastic Business." In *Medieval Women and the Sources of Medieval History*, edited by Joel T. Rosenthal. Athens: University of Georgia Press, 1990.

Greven, Joseph. *Die Anfänge der Beginen: Ein Beitrag zur Geschichte der Volksfrommigkeit und des Ordenswesens im Hochmittelalter.* Vorreformationsgeschichtliche Forschungen 8. Munster: Aschendorff, 1912.

Grundmann, Herbert. *Religiöse Bewegungen im Mittelalter.* Berlin: E. Ebering, 1935.

Harline, Craig. "Actives and Contemplatives: The Female Religious of the Low Countries Before and After Trent." *The Catholic Historical Review* 89, no. 4 (1995) 541–67.

Helmholz, Richard. *Canon Law and the Law of England.* London: Hambledon Press, 1987.

———. *Roman Canon Law in Reformation England.* Cambridge: Cambridge University Press, 1990.

Herde, Peter. *Cölestin V (1294) (Peter von Morrone) der Engelpapst.* Stuttgart: Anton Hiersemann, 1981.

Horwitz, Steven. "Magistri and Magisterium: Saint Raymond of Penyafort and the Gregoriana." *Escritos del Vedat* 7 (1977): 209–38.

Houlbrooke, Ralph. *Church Courts and the People during the English Reformation 1520–1570.* Oxford: Oxford University Press, 1979.

Huyghe, Gerard. *La clôture des moniales des origines à la fin du XIIIe siècle.* Roubaix, 1944.

Jelsma, Auke. "The Appreciation of Bridget of Sweden (1303–1373) in the 15th Century." In *Women and Men in Spiritual Culture XIV–XVII C,* edited by Schulte and Kessel. The Hague, 1986.

Johnson, Penelope. *Equal in Monastic Profession.* Chicago: University of Chicago Press, 1991.

Jombart, Emil, and Marcel Viller. "Clôture." *Dictionnaire de Spiritualité.* Vol. II (Paris, 1953) 979–1007.

Jordan, W. C. "The Cistercian Nunnery of La Cour Notre-Dame de Michery: A House That Failed." *Revue Bénédictine* 95 (1985): 311–20.

Knowles, David. *Bare Ruined Choirs.* London: Cambridge University Press, 1976.

Koch, Gottfried. *Frauenfrage und Ketzertum im Mittelalter: Die Frauenbewegung im Rahmen des Katharismus und des Waldensertums und ihre sozialen Wurzeln: 12.– 14. Jahrhundert.* Forschungen zur mittelalterlichen Geschichte 9. Berlin: Akademie-Verlag, 1962.

Koorn, Florence. "Women without Vows." In *Women and Men in Spiritual Culture XIV–XVII C,* edited by Schulte and Kessel. The Hague, 1986.

Kuttner, Stephan. "Research on Gratian: Acta and Agenda." *Proceedings of the Seventh International Congress of Medieval Canon Law,* edited by Peter Linehan, pp. 3–26. Città del Vaticano: Biblioteca Apostolica Vaticana, 1988.

———. "The Revival of Jurisprudence." In *Renaissance and Renewal in the Twelfth*

144   Bibliography

Century, edited by Robert Benson and Giles Constable. Cambridge: Cambridge University Press, 1982.

Lainati, Sr. Chiara Augusta. "La clôture de Sainte Claire et des premières Clarisses dans la législation canonique et dans la pratique." *Laurentianum* 14 (1973): 223–50.

Lambert, Malcolm. *Medieval Heresy: Popular Movements from Bogomil to Hus.* New York: Holmes and Meier, 1977.

Lawrence, C. H. *Medieval Monasticism.* London, 1984.

Le Bourgeois, Sr. Marie-Amélie. "Dieu aime-t-il les murs?" *Le Supplément* 137 (1986): 19–38.

Le Bras, Gabriel, C. Lefebvre, and J. Rambaud. *L'Age classique 1140–1378: Sources et théorie du droit.* Histoire du droit et des institutions de l'église en occident. Vol. 7. Paris, 1965.

LeClerq, Jean. "La Clôture." *Collectanea Cisterciensia* 43 (1981): 366–76.

———. "Medieval Feminine Monasticism: Reality vs. Romantic Images." *Benedictus: Studies in Honor of St. Benedict of Nursia.* Studies in Medieval Cistercian History 8. Kalamazoo: Cistercian Publications, 1981.

Lekai, L. J. *The Cistercians: Ideals and Reality.* Kent, Ohio: Kent State University Press, 1977.

Lerner, Robert. *The Heresy of the Free Spirit in the Later Middle Ages.* Berkeley: University of California Press, 1972.

Logan, F. Donald. "The First Royal Visitation of the English Universities, 1535." *English Historical Review* 106 (1991): 861–89.

———. *Runaway Religious in England, c. 1240–1540.* Cambridge Studies in Medieval Life and Thought: Fourth Series 32. New York: Cambridge University Press, 1996.

Lynch, Joseph. *Simoniacal Entry into Religious Life from 1000 to 1260: A Social, Economic and Legal Study.* Columbus: Ohio State University Press, 1976.

McCarthy, Mother Maria Caritas. *The Rule for Nuns of St. Caesarius of Arles.* Washington: The Catholic University of America Press, 1960.

McDonnell, Ernest. *The Beguines and Beghards in Medieval Culture.* New Brunswick, N.J.: Rutgers University Press, 1954.

McLaughlin, Eleanor. "Les Femmes et l'hérésie médiévale: Un Problème dans l'histoire de la spiritualité." *Concilium* 111 (1976): 73–90.

McNamara, Jo Ann. "De Quibusdam Mulieribus: Reading Womens' History from Hostile Sources." In *Women and the Sources of Medieval History,* edited by Joel Rosenthal, pp. 237–58. Athens, Ga.: University of Georgia Press, 1990.

Mollat, Michel. *The Poor in the Middle Ages.* Translated by Arthur Goldhammer. New Haven: Yale University Press, 1978.

Moore, R. I. *The Origins of European Dissent.* New York: St. Martin's Press, 1977.

———. *The Formation of a Persecuting Society: Power and Deviance in Western Europe 950–1250.* Oxford and New York: Basil Blackwell, 1987.

Muldoon, James. "Boniface VIII's Forty Years of Experience in the Law." *The Jurist* 31 (1971): 449–77.

Nichols, John. "English Cistercian Nuns." In *Distant Echoes.* Vol. 1, edited by John A. Nichols and Lilian Thomas Shank. Cistercian Studies Series 71. Kalamazoo, Mich: Cistercian Publications, 1984.

Noonan, John T. "Gratian Slept Here: The Changing Identity of the Father of the Systematic Study of the Canon Law." *Traditio* 35 (1979): 145–72.

Owen, Dorothy. "An Episcopal Audience Court." In *Legal Records and the Historian*, edited by J. H. Baker, pp. 140–49. London: Royal Historical Society, 1978.

———. *The Medieval Canon Law.* Cambridge: Cambridge University Press, 1990.

Parisse, Michel. *Les Nonnes au Moyen Age.* Le Puy: Christine Bonneton, 1983.

Pennington, Kenneth. *The Prince and the Law, 1200–1600: Sovereignty and Rights in the Western Legal Tradition.* Berkeley: University of California Press, 1993.

Petroff, Elizabeth. *Medieval Women's Visionary Literature.* Oxford: Oxford University Press, 1986.

Post, Gaines. *Studies in Medieval Legal Thought.* Princeton: Princeton University Press, 1964.

Power, Eileen. *Medieval English Nunneries.* Cambridge: Cambridge University Press, 1922.

Raine, James. ed. *Depositions and other Ecclesiastical Proceedings of the Courts of Durham Extending from 1311 to the Reign of Elizabeth.* London: Surtees Society Publications, 1847.

Rambaud-Buhot, Jacqueline. *Le statut des moniales chez les Pères de l'église, dans les règles monastiques et les collections canoniques jusqu'au XIIe siècle.* Paris, 1956.

Rodriguez, F. Cantelar. "El apparatus de Bernardo Raimondo al Libro Sexto de Bonifacio VIII." *Proceedings of the Fifth International Congress of Medieval Canon Law,* pp. 213–58. Città del Vaticano: Biblioteca Apostolica Vaticana, 1980.

Rosenwein, Barbara, and Lester Little. "Social Meaning in Monastic and Mendicant Spiritualities." *Past and Present* 63 (1974): 4–32.

Schmidt, Tilmann. "Bonifaz VIII als Gesetzgeber: Der Liber Sextus von 1298 und die bonifazianischen Extravaganten." *Monumenta Iuris Canonici Subsidia* 9, pp. 227–46. Città del Vaticano: Biblioteca Apostolica Vaticana, 1992.

Schulenburg, Jane Tibbetts. "Strict Active Enclosure and Its Effects on the Female Monastic Experience ca. 500–1100." In *Distant Echoes: Medieval Religious Women,* I, edited by J. A. Nichols and L. T. Shank, pp. 51–86. Kalamazoo, Mich.: Cistercian Publications, 1984.

Simons, Walter. "The Beguine Movement in the Southern Low Countries: A Reassessment." *Bulletin de l'Institut Historique Belge de Rome* 59 (1989): 63–105.

Southern, R. W. *Western Society and the Church in the Middle Ages.* Harmondsworth: Penguin, 1970.

Strayer, Joseph. *The Reign of Philip the Fair.* Princeton: Princeton University Press, 1980.

Thompson, Sally. "The Problem of the Cistercian Nuns in the Twelfth and Early Thirteenth Centuries." In *Medieval Women,* edited by Derek Baker, pp. 227–52. Studies in Church History, Subsidia I. Oxford: B. Blackwell for the Ecclesiastical Historical Society, 1978.

Tierney, Brian. "Canon Law and Church Institutions in the Late Middle Ages." *Proceedings of the Seventh International Congress of Medieval Canon Law,* edited by Peter Linehan, pp. 49–69. Città del Vaticano: Biblioteca Apostolica Vaticana, 1988.

————. *The Crisis of Church and State.* Englewood Cliffs, N.J.: Prentice Hall, 1964.

Ullmann, Walter. *Law and Politics in the Middle Ages.* London: The Sources of History Limited, 1975.

Watson, Alan. *Roman Law and Comparative Law.* Athens, Ga.: University of Georgia Press, 1991.

Wemple, Suzanne. *Women in Frankish Society: Marriage and the Cloister 500–900.* Philadelphia: University of Pennsylvania Press, 1981.

Wessley, Stephen E. "The Thirteenth-Century Guglielmites: Salvation through Women." In *Medieval Women,* edited by Derek Baker, pp. 289–303. Oxford: Basil Blackwell, 1978.

Williman, Daniel. "A Liber Sextus from the Bonifacian Library." *Bulletin of Medieval Canon Law* 7 (1977): 103–8.

Wilts, Andreas. *Beginen im Bodenseeraum.* Sigmaringen: Jan Thorbecke, 1994.

Wood, Charles, ed. and trans. *Philip the Fair and Boniface VIII.* New York, 1967.

Woodcock, Brian. *Medieval Ecclesiastical Courts in the Diocese of Canterbury.* Oxford: Oxford University Press, 1952.

Wunderli, Richard M. *London Church Courts on the Eve of the Reformation.* Cambridge: Medieval Academy of America Publications, 1981.

Index

147

Canon Law and Cloistered Women was composed in Meridien by Brevis Press, Bethany, Connecticut; printed on 60-pound Glatfelter by Cushing-Malloy, Inc., Ann Arbor, Michigan; bound by John Dekker & Sons, Grand Rapids, Michigan; and designed and produced by Kachergis Book Design, Pittsboro, North Carolina.

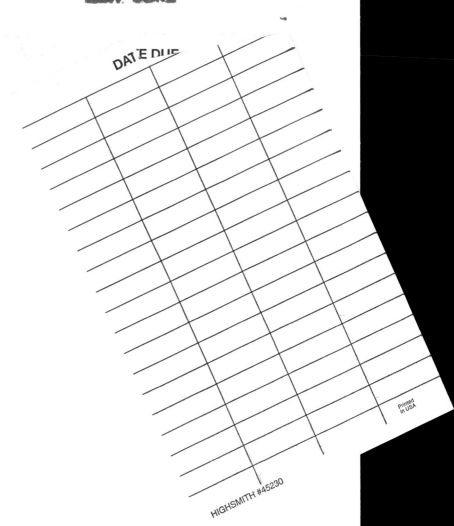

DATE DUE

HIGHSMITH #45230

Printed
in USA